Joyce Storey

The Thames and Hudson
Manual of **Textile**
Printing

Revised Edition

with 160 illustrations, in colour and black and white

Thames and Hudson 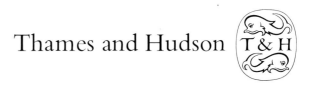 T & H

PHOTOGRAPHIC
ACKNOWLEDGMENTS

Acknowledgments are due to the
following for permission to
reproduce the pictures on the pages
shown:

American Museum, Bath, 59 (top
and bottom left), 64; British
Museum, 19 (2); Cranko
Engineering Co. Ltd., 115, 123;
David Evans & Co. Ltd., 36, 38
(bottom); Miss Joan Evans, 33 (top);
Faculty of Art and Design,
Manchester Polytechnic, 22, 40, 83
(right); Charles Griffin & Co.
(publishers of *The Principles and
Practice of Textile Printing* by E.
Knecht and J. B. Fothergill), and the
authors, 58, 59 (bottom right);
Liberty & Co. Ltd., 127 (top);
Jocelyn Morton, 108; Musée de
l'Impression sur Etoffes de
Mulhouse, 54 (bottom), 62; Paisley
Museum, 45, 48; Science Museum,
32, 34 (right); Victoria and Albert
Museum, 10, 13, 15 (2), 16
(bottom), 23, 28, 35, 60, 63, 65, 68,
69, 109, 111, 180; Whitworth Art
Gallery, University of Manchester,
25, 26, 51, 52, 101 (top), 103 (top),
127 (bottom); William Morris
Gallery, Walthamstow, 33 (right),
178 (2), 179 (2).

First published in Great Britain
in 1974
First paperback edition 1979
Revised edition 1992

© 1974 and 1992 Thames and
Hudson Ltd, London

Printed and bound in Singapore by
CS Graphics

To W. Frank Uhlig

AND HUDSON MANUALS

GENERAL EDITOR: W.S. TAYLOR

Textile Printing

Contents

Preface to the Revised Edition

In this edition, I have taken the opportunity to update text and illustrations in the light of major developments since the first printing, and I have written a new chapter (Chapter 8) summarizing the advance of computer-based technology into the 1990s. Where developmental trends are discussed elsewhere in the text, these refer to the state-of-the-art in 1974, when this book was first published. Where appropriate, additions to the text show how these trends have progressed. My thanks are especially due to Stork (Boxmeer); Zedco (UK); Sci-Tex (Israel); Ciba-Geigy (Basel); and many other people and companies who so readily gave their help and supplied new material.

I would also like to thank my colleagues at the Philadelphia College of Textiles and Science, where I have been teaching design and textile printing technology since 1978, and my friends in the American textile industry – in particular Frank Uhlig, John Ogletree Snr and Phil Salaff – printers and textile chemists who from my first days in the States introduced me to all sections of the print industry and to the A.A.T.C.C. (American Association of Textile Chemists and Colorists). I was invited to join the Printing Technology Committee (RA80) and latterly became Chairman of the group. I have also taken students to Europe several times and have received wonderful help and friendship from many people at Stork, Arioli, Buser, Ciba-Geigy (Basel) and many others. These experiences have all contributed to my knowledge and that of my students.

JOYCE STOREY (1991)

Introduction

This manual, primarily intended for design students in polytechnics and colleges, will trace the evolution of fabric printing techniques from the earliest 'resist' painting to the latest highly sophisticated machine-produced screen and transfer work. It is not intended to be a history, but only to show the interrelationship of history and methods of printing. Historical methods will be discussed in detail only where they have a direct bearing on the understanding of modern processes or where (as in engraved roller printing) the methods are in essence exactly the same as when first introduced. The book will, however, be concerned only with the various devices, tools, and machines used to create pattern in dye on cloth. I will not touch, in any detail, on cloth preparation, dyes, thickenings, finishing processes or discharges; these will be the subject of a second volume.

The first contact with industry, for design students, is

nearly always a 'works visit', and great numbers of students find excitement and interest in seeing the methods demonstrated. But perhaps almost more important, they meet people who, although possibly good-humouredly poking fun at art students, are prepared to give endless time and trouble to the task of explaining complicated processes, and who display immense patience and kindness while doing so.

My hope is that this book will help to make such a visit more understandable both before and afterwards, as well as providing detailed information to enable the student to tackle some of the methods himself. But above all, I hope that it will go some way towards bridging the gap between college and industry: this seems to me to be as vital today as it was in the past. My one big fear about it – aside from the obvious difficulty of putting over simplified explanations of highly involved processes – has been that because it is a manual or textbook, it would succeed in being purely informative without inspiring interest. For the reason why I agreed to write it – after recognizing that there was a very real need for an up-to-date, well-illustrated book of this type – was because, as a designer and teacher of design for many years, I have found a growing fascination not only in the skills both inherited and newly learnt, and in the various processes, but in printworks in general, coupled with a high regard for all the people involved. I firmly believe that mutual liking, respect and understanding are the only basis on which a creative and well-trained design student can become a good and useful designer.

One of the enjoyable features of writing this book has been the co-operation I have received so unstintingly from everyone I approached, whether museums, factories, trade and research organizations or private individuals. I could not have received more genuine kindness or interest and it would certainly not have been possible to produce the book without such help. As well as those mentioned below there were many people whose names I never found out, but who have been equally helpful; I would like to thank them and also anyone I may have unwittingly left out.

First, my thanks are due to my Head of Department at Manchester Polytechnic, Mr R. E. R. Downing ARCA, for suggesting that I might like to write the book and for help and encouragement in writing it. For permission to have photographs taken I should like to thank: at the Whitworth Art Gallery, Manchester, Professor C. R. Dodwell and Mrs Joan Allgrove (also for much help and advice); at the William Morris Gallery, Walthamstow, the Curator; at the Paisley Museum, Mr David R. Shearer; at the American Museum in Britain, Mrs. E. M. Gonin, Assistant Curator; and at the Victoria and Albert Museum Indian Study room, Miss Tyas (for her assistance). I am also grateful to the many firms who have supplied photographs and given help through technical representatives: Mr. H. Ellis (Peter

Zimmer Kufstein); Mr Flood (Johannes Zimmer, Klagenfurt); Mr Dennis Kershaw (Fritz Buser, Switzerland); Mr C.A. Crowther (Stork, Boxmeer); Saueressig, Ahaus; Mr E.P. Furlong (Mather & Platt, Manchester); English Calico Ltd. – Mr J.H. Schofield (for permission to have photographs taken) and the managers and staff at Levenshulme Engraving works, Strines printworks, Loveclough printworks and Dinting Engineering, for many hours of help; Mr W.W. Sword (Aljaba Ltd); Mr S.J. Cox (Cobden Chadwick Ltd, Oldham); Mr Armstrong (Cranco Engineering Ltd, Nottingham); Mr Sherratt (Barracks Fabrics Printing Co. Ltd, Macclesfield); the Directors of Park Adam Ltd, Macclesfield; Mr C.S. Brooks (David Evans & Co. Ltd, Crayford); Mr G.V. Lowe, Mr Woolgar, Mr Bryson and many others of Arthur Sanderson & Sons Ltd, Uxbridge; Liberty & Co. – the manager and staff of Merton printworks and the public relations department; Mr Neff and Mr C.F. Jackson (British Silk Dyeing Co. Ltd); Mr Pat Marriott, now of Milne & Yates; Mrs Ada Lowit, for the use of cloth samples, and Mr W.S. Boston and staff at the Society of Dyers and Colourists, Bradford for the loan of valuable old books and permission to quote from the Society's Journals; Mr M.A. Buckley and others of M.A. Buckley (Engravers) Warrington (also for permission to have photographs taken); Mr Leese and others (Bemrose Ltd); Mr Goodier and Mr Holt (Screentex Ltd, St Helen's); Charles Griffin & Co. Ltd, for permission to use diagrams from *The Principles and Practice of Textile Printing* by Knecht and Fothergill; Mr Jocelyn Morton for photographs and permission to quote from his book *Three Generations in a Family Textile Firm*. Finally, my thanks go to Mr Stephen Yates and Mr Terry Waddington, both of Manchester Polytechnic, for taking the photographs, and to Mr W.S. Taylor and the staff of Thames and Hudson for all the understanding, help and useful criticism they gave to enable the book to be completed.

Resist print in blue from about the fifth century. The scene represents the
Nativity, with the Angel in attendance on the Virgin. Found at the
burial-grounds at Akhmin, Upper Egypt.

1 Beginnings of textile printing

The term 'textile printing' is rather an ambiguous one which, for the purpose of this book, is used to indicate the patterning of cloth by means of printing, dyeing or painting. It is possible to divide printed fabrics into four different classes or styles: the 'resist' style, the 'dyed' (or mordant) style, the 'discharge' style and the 'direct' style. Of these, the first two are by far the oldest. All four styles can obviously be used in conjunction with a great variety of devices, from the simplest brush or thread, as in 'tie-and-dye', to the most elaborate and sophisticated of modern screenprinting machinery. It is the exploration of these devices and the development of all the ingenious aids for imparting pattern to cloth that is my main concern in this book.

Man's urge to decorate his clothing and the fabrics of his environment, by means of printing, dates from the very earliest times, and fabrics so patterned existed before woven or embroidered ones. For, although the earliest examples extant are from the fifth- to sixth-century Coptic period in Egypt, various records show that printed fabric did exist about 2500 BC. Patterned garments are shown on wall-paintings in Egyptian tombs and Herodotus mentions similar findings in the Caucasus of 2000 BC. Whether the people of China or India were the first to make simple blocks for the printing of cotton cloth, it seems certain that textile printing was a fairly extensive industry in India during the earliest part of the Christian era.

The resist style

The principle of this method is that the pattern area is painted or stamped with a 'resist' made from rice paste, clay or some type of wax. Then the cloth is dyed, so leaving the pattern areas reserved in white against a dyed background. As far as the Coptic cloths were concerned, the patterns were stamped with small blocks in geometric shapes, several being used in different combinations, the fabric then being passed through a dye-bath of woad, indigo or other blue dye. There are also Coptic fabrics which were painted with resist.

The dyed style

Here also dyeing was used, but this time in conjunction with a 'mordant'. The colouring matter obtained from animal and vegetable sources needs to be used in conjunction with a

* For further details about types of
mordants, see p. 173

fixing agent (mordant), usually in the form of a metallic oxide or acetate, in order to make the dye insoluble when washing and fast when exposed to light. When the cloth was dyed, only those areas of pattern so painted took the colour, the mordant and vegetable colouring matter forming an insoluble colour after fixing in the open air, and the unmordanted parts washing clear and clean in water.*

The discharge style

Comparatively recently, in the early part of the nineteenth century, it was discovered that it was possible by chemical means to bleach out or 'discharge' a pattern from an already piece-dyed cloth. This discharging process enabled fairly intricate and fine patterns to be printed, giving the effect of resist dyeing. Subsequently, these white areas could be reprinted in colour. (Nowadays colour discharges are produced in which a range of dyestuffs unaffected by the discharging agent are added to the discharge paste, so while the one is taking out the colour of the dyed ground, the other is being deposited in its place.)

The direct style

Until the advent of chemically produced dyestuffs there was very little direct printing (that is, printing with a paste containing both the colour and the fixing agent). The exceptions were almost all pigment colours. These colours, unlike dyestuffs which stain the fibre of the cloth, merely coat the outside of each warp and weft thread they contact.

At this point it is interesting to look at the two earliest styles in greater detail and for this purpose a study of Javanese batiks and Indian palampores provides the most beautiful and accomplished examples. I shall also touch briefly on 'tie-and-dye' as practised in India.

JAVANESE BATIKS

Batik work is found in South-east Asia, India, Europe and Africa, but it reached its highest development in Java. The word is possibly derived from the root *tik*, which is thought to be an onomatopoeic word meaning 'drop' or 'dot'. From records of the Sung Dynasty (960–1279), we find that batiked cotton cloth from Java was very highly prized and made presents for princes.

For many centuries, the designs and quality remained unchanged, being practised only by the Javanese women and girls of the upper classes and the nobility. It was the tradition of these families to pass on the inherited skills and ideas and it was not until the second half of the nineteenth century that batik making began to be organized as a home

Javanese batik, showing contrasted design qualities superbly related on
one piece of cloth.

Tjantings: (*top*) the old type, still made and used, virtually unchanged, in Java; (*above*) a modern Malaysian type.

industry. In recent years, however, instruction in the skills of batik designing and waxing has been started in training establishments set up by the government in an effort to preserve all that is best in these traditional fabrics.

Among the Javanese women the old-style garments are still worn a great deal, whereas the men adopt Western dress for everyday use and reserve their patterned cottons for special occasions. The chief garments are the *sarong* (a rectangular cloth sewn into a tube and worn wrapped round the waist from hips to ankles); the *pandjang* (a long cloth, longer than the *sarong*); and the *slendang* (a long, narrow shawl). Since about 1815 Java has imported cotton from India and it is always measured, cut and sewn before the batik work begins.

First, the cloth has to be made completely free from size and grease before work commences, by boiling and washing. Next, it is treated with a mordant of oil and lye, a substance obtained from the bark of trees. This is a long process, especially if red dye is used. To prevent the liquid wax spreading too much the cloth is then sized with dilute rice or cassava paste and then pounded with a wooden mallet to make it smooth and supple.

From now on the women take over – all the wax painting and designing is still the female prerogative. They put in the main lines of the design with charcoal, this being done in greater or lesser detail according to the skill and experience of the particular designer. The experienced worker relies on memory and instinct when adding details within the framework of the design.

The wax is heated and applied with an instrument called a *tjanting*. Used exclusively in Java, it consists of a copper cup with one or more spouts, fastened to a reed or bamboo handle. For producing groups of spots, double lines, rosettes, etc., numbers of spouts are used. Small spaces are filled in with larger spouts and bigger areas with a brush.

To facilitate the waxing process the cloth is stretched over a bamboo frame and the wax kept hot on a small charcoal stove. When one side of the cloth has been waxed it is turned over and rewaxed, this time on the reverse side. Skilful handling is required to keep the wax flowing evenly, and the women have to blow continually on the opening of the spout to keep it clear. Line work (of which there is a great deal) needs very pure wax of the best quality, but the inside shapes can be put in using cheaper mixtures.

Once the wax application is complete the whole cloth is dipped into a cold dye-bath and it remains immersed until sufficient depth of colour has been absorbed by the unprotected parts of the cloth. In recent years, vegetable dyes have been almost entirely superseded by aniline colours, first introduced in 1900, although they are still used in a small percentage of the special work.

After dyeing and drying, part of the layer of wax is carefully peeled off with a knife, revealing the white cloth

Two more examples of Javanese batik.

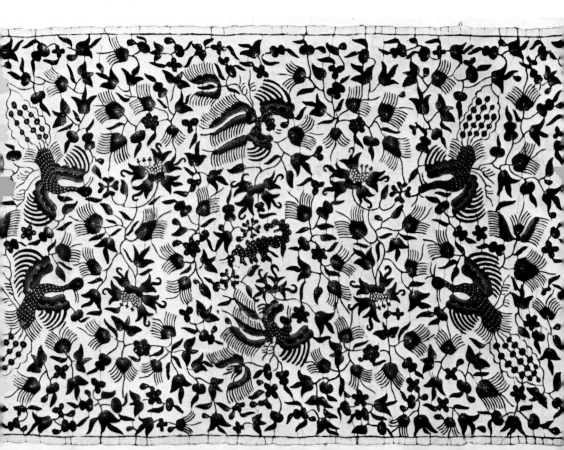

underneath. Another layer of wax is then applied to protect any parts of the design needing to be kept in the first dye colour (usually a deep blue). The cloth is then immersed in a second dye-bath, often containing soga brown (a vegetable colour from an Indonesian plant). Thus the resulting pattern is in dark blue, rich brown and bluish black.

The wax is finally removed from the cloth by melting in boiling water, and the fabric is then glazed by being rubbed and polished with a shell.

Although a batik *sarong* about two yards long would have taken, and still takes when hand-painted, at least thirty or forty days to make, the cloth which emerges is so rich in colouring and pattern, so smooth and supple to handle (and is also completely reversible), that one cannot possibly feel that the time matters at all.

Modern batiks

In the home industry and training schools the work is ordered and planned carefully, using the varying skills and experience of the different people involved, both beginners and those with greater ability, to produce a more mechanical version of the traditional designs.

In about 1850 the first attempts were made to simplify and speed up the production of batiks, and waxing by means of blocks, or *tjap* printing, was started. These blocks consist of strips of soldered copper, and are open at the back. The wax was transferred to the block by means of a thick pad of cloth made rather like the ink-pad used for rubber stamping. This method means that about twenty *sarongs* can be made ready for dyeing in one day and, unlike the hand waxing, it is done entirely by the men.

Another quick method is the use of lacquered paper stencils to apply a resist paste of groundnuts. This use of stencils will be referred to later, in the chapter on screen printing (see p. 110). A number of batiks have a crackled effect in some of the colours, produced deliberately by

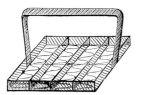

The back of a nineteenth-century *tjap* printing block.

Another *tjap* block, this time of a *parang* pattern. *Parang*, meaning 'rugged rock' or 'crag', is the diagonal band design so often seen in Javanese work.

A *tjap* printing block in the form of an exotic butterfly, showing how these special blocks were (and still are) made of strips of metal soldered together without any backing of wood.

The reverse side of the *tjap* butterfly, enlarged to show the conglomeration of metal strips, and part of the handle and the thicker pieces of metal which constitute the only support.

A modern Indian silk chiffon scarf with a 'tie-and-dye' pattern. The fashion recently has been to leave the fabric unsmoothed, so that the nail marks and raised points of cloth show up.

hardening the wax layer in a bath of very cold water prior to dyeing, and crushing the cloth together to cause small fissures in the wax, which allow the dye to seep through. The crackled effect is considered desirable in the soga brown, but with indigo care is taken to prevent it happening by slightly softening the resist in the sun.

INDIAN TIE-AND-DYE OR BANDHANA WORK

Tie-dyeing is a native craft practised in many countries all over the world, with possibly the best examples coming from India and Africa. The Indian bandhana work is especially interesting because not only are the cottons and silks produced in this way so lovely, but they gave their name and also the idea for a resist process to nineteenth-century England; the tramp's red spotted handkerchief is a product of that period and is a bandhana too. The women in Indian villages who work in this way are known as *bandhanaris*.

This is another resist technique, in which certain parts of the cloth remain undyed because they have been covered by 'tied threads' and knots. Small seeds or shells can be fastened into the cloth; it can be pleated and then tied; large areas of it can be gathered together, forming great variegated 'sunbursts' of colour; and countless other simple or more complicated methods can be used to produce a wealth of different effects, all of which are characterized by more or less softening, or bleeding, of the colour at the edges of the shapes.

First, the material is folded several times until it is reduced to a square or rectangular piece many folds in thickness. The cloth is then dampened and pressed on to a block on which the designer has put a pattern in pointed nails.

In order to make it easier to gather up small pieces of the cloth and tie it round with string at the points where the

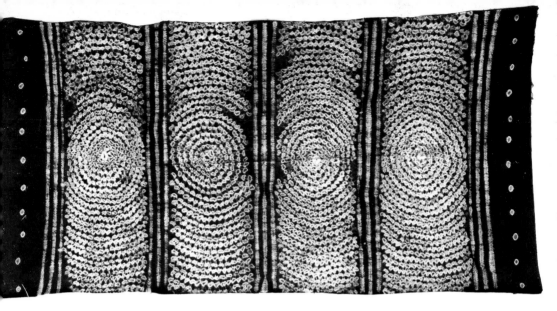

Two different types of African 'tie-and-dye': (*above*) seeds have been used to create a pattern; (*below*) the cloth has been pleated before dyeing.

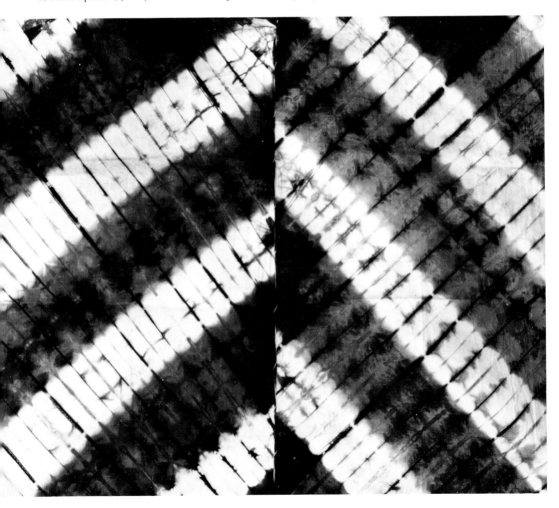

nails have been, the women grow the finger-nails of their thumbs and forefingers very long, thereby making them act like a pair of pincers. Sometimes they rub a resist paste on the string first, but often it is quite sufficient to tie untreated threads as the tightness of the strings acts as a barrier to the dye. These threads are not cut between each point but carried along from one nail-mark to another. The cloth is then dyed in the lightest colour and the process repeated, either after undoing the first set of threads, or, if white is part of the design, these are left in and a new set of threads added to the pattern. When finished the cloth used to be stretched and smoothed, but in recent examples the pointed creasing round the nail-marks is left in as part of the style of the finished silk.

INDIAN PALAMPORES IN EUROPE

Cotton had been woven in India since long before Christ, but it was under the great Moghul Dynasty (1525–1707) that the beautiful cotton muslins reached their highest development. Although silk had been cultivated and woven from the very earliest times it was the fine cotton cloths that were by far the most prized. Dacca muslins known by such exotic names as Running Water, Woven Air and Evening Dew were so fine that a turban cloth 1 yard wide and 20 yards long could be passed through a finger-ring.

Indian hand-painted cottons came to Europe in the late sixteenth and early seventeenth centuries, along with other cargoes such as spices, perfumes and embroideries. At first England tended to get them at second hand by raiding the Spanish and Portuguese ships, then in 1631 the East India Company was set up and given permission to import these painted 'calicoes' or 'chints' (from the Hindu word *chint* meaning 'coloured' or 'variegated').

Their colours and designs so fired the imagination of people in France, Holland, Portugal and England that the competition to bring back the finest examples available defied all bans and prohibitions. The rich at court and else-where tried to outdo each other in the wearing and using of these painted fabrics. Gradually, besides encouraging the Indians to blockprint as well as paint their fabrics for greater speed (printing from blocks was an old-established craft in India), people in England and in other European countries started to try to produce simple copies of the Indian patterns using rather crudely cut blocks and half-learnt Indian dyeing techniques.

In any book on printed textiles, whether a history or a manual, no excuse could be necessary for including Indian hand-painted cottons, for they are among the most beautiful painted or printed fabrics ever made, or ever likely to be made. But aside from this, there are at least three other very good and cogent reasons for dwelling on them a little. First, the Indian work formed the basis of dress fabric and furnishing designs throughout Europe in the seventeenth and eighteenth centuries, and floral styles of sprigs, bouquets and trails are still used in varying forms today. Second, the desire for similar cottons, if the originals were not available, brought about the start of the European textile industries. And third, the Indian and Middle Eastern madder technique of producing a range of colours in conjunction with various mordants became the basis of the European dye systems, for it was the analysis of alizarin, the colouring matter in the madder plant, and the subsequent chemical reproduction of it, that paved the way for most later experiments in dye chemistry. Although dyes of vegetable colouring matter in conjunction with 'drugs', or mordants, had been used in Europe for a long period, it was nevertheless the keen appreciation of the Indian cottons which acted as an incentive to much deeper investigations and analysis.

When cottons were first brought over to Europe they were used mainly for bedcoverings – 'palampores', as they were called (also sometimes 'palampost' or 'palangosh'). There were two main kinds of palampores: those usually without a border, and with the 'Tree of Life' in the centre, which were used for bedhangings, and those with borders and a formal pattern in the centre and used for bedspreads because of their two-way design. The other form of the Tree of Life symbol was the 'pinecone', or seed with the tree inside. This last was the original of the much-used 'Paisley' shape, so called by reason of its adoption as the main motif of the shawls woven at Paisley, in Scotland, in the nineteenth century in imitation of the silk and Kashmiri ones.

The cloth was first smoothed and burnished to give it a fine surface. This was done with buffalo milk instead of size. Next, the design was outlined on paper, then holes were pierced along the main lines and powdered charcoal was rubbed through these, so transferring the design to the cloth. The outlines of the red flowers and the black lines were then painted in.

After this, all the parts which were required to be blue or green were left blank and the rest of the cloth was waxed to reserve it. The cloth was then dipped in a bath of indigo dye. This elaborate process was necessary because indigo was not fast unless it was applied in the form of a dye-bath rather than by printing or painting. The wax was removed by scraping and then washing.

Next came the painstaking process of painting in all the flowers and birds and stems. This was done with a variety of different mordants – acetates of iron, alum, chrome, zinc and tin, which in combination with the colouring matter from the madder plant gave the fabric its rich range of colours: black, brown, crimson, purple, lilac and pink. The cloth was immersed in the madder dye-bath and the various colours would emerge simultaneously. Any extra details

Eighteenth-century Indian
blockprinted cotton.

within the shapes were then waxed in and a redyeing took
place. Washing the cotton fabric got rid of almost all the
dye from the unmordanted areas, the ground becoming
clear, and the dyes fast, when the material was spread in
the fields and subjected to the lightening and bleaching
effects of the sun and air. (This fixing process subsequently
became known as 'ageing'.) Last, small yellow areas were
painted in – on the white cloth and also over any parts of the
blue which were to be made greenish. The dye is not known
for certain but may be saffron. As this painted dye was not
very fast, it has nearly all disappeared.

Masulipatam was probably the most important centre for
this work; it was famous as early as the first century AD for
painted fabrics. The Dutch, who were the first to establish a
trading centre there, in 1615 started a factory which they
later abandoned, only to re-establish it in 1631 when the city
also became the centre of English trade.

In 1686 the trade reached a peak, and one can get some
idea of its vastness from the fact that even seven years later,
in 1693, orders at one factory alone reached 17,000, partly
in piece goods and partly in palampores – and there were
scores of centres. Another important feature noticed in the
orders is that from the beginning of the eighteenth century
there was an increasing use of the word 'printed', which
establishes beyond doubt that from this time the use of
blocks in the chintz industry was common practice.

The years 1731 to 1740 saw a great deal of European
influence but one order contains the injunction: 'Let the

Indians work their own fancies, which is always preferable before any patterns we can send you from Europe.' In 1740, smaller patterns were much more in demand and were used a great deal for dresses. But from this time there was a gradual falling-off in the trade in painted and printed cottons and more orders for 'Patna cloth in white state' to be used for printing in England. There was a drop in standard of the work, too, in the early 1750s, no doubt brought about by too much pressure and coercion, and in 1753 the chintz trade as a regular industry had virtually ceased.

The most thorough and detailed knowledge of the involved methods used by the Indians was provided in 1742 by Father Cœurdoux, a Jesuit missionary at Pondicherry. He

Eighteenth-century Indian hand-painted fabric for the Dutch market.

23

wrote very minute instructions, after being repeatedly asked to do so by a friend in France. These revealed not only the painstaking Indian techniques but also the extremely thorough research work of the priest. The letters must have been kept secret for about thirty years; they certainly helped the French to forge ahead with much greater knowledge and were thought for many years to be the main reason for apparent French supremacy in the field.

This brief history and the outline description of the methods involved say nothing of the skill, patience and complete unconcern for the passing of time that must have been so much a part of the way of life of the craftsmen of the time. Above all it is possible to give only an idea of the love of colour and the feeling for flowers and growing plants, birds and animals, and indeed for the cycle of life itself, symbolized in the Trees of Life and the mountains and flowing streams with which they are all patterned so richly. Go and see the fabrics themselves, and the experience will be one never to be forgotten, and immensely humbling for any designer. The Victoria and Albert Museum in London and the Whitworth Art Gallery in Manchester have superb collections, as do the Cooper-Hewitt Museum in New York, the Textile Museum in Washington and the Royal Ontario Museum, Toronto.

In 1708 Daniel Defoe wrote sarcastically of the situation:

We saw our Persons of Quality dress'd in Indian carpets, which but a few Years before their Chamber maids would have thought too ordinary; the Chints were advanc'd from lying on the Floor to their Back, from Foot-Cloth to Petticoat, . . . nor was this all, but it crept into our Houses, our closets, and Bed-chambers, Curtains, Cushions, Chairs, . . . in short, everything that used to be wool or silk . . . supplied by Indian trade. What remained for our people to do but to stand still and look on, see the Bread taken out of their Mouths and the East India trade carry away the whole Employment of their People?

But, to quote a more recent writer in the *CIBA Review*:

instead of standing still and looking on, the British invented the factory system. Soon the flow of cheap cottons was reversed and before long it was English fabrics that were depriving Indian weavers of their livelihood. Then, in recent decades, the flow of goods again switched from East to West; the factory system had been adopted in the Far East.

The sad thing is that when in the 1920s G. P. Baker did the research for his still unsurpassed survey of Indian chintz, he tried to find evidence of the industry lingering on, and by showing the illustrations of old fabrics sought to recall memories of similar work and methods in the minds of the older people, but failed to do so. In the end all we have managed to do is to kill most of the native skill and to pass on the factory system.

(*Opposite*) Javanese batik belt (late nineteenth century). The ground is of cream cotton, with a narrow batik border and a stylized two-headed bird at either end.

2 Block printing

Before embarking on a detailed account of the various methods used in the making of blocks, it is necessary to trace briefly the history of early printing by this method in the Far East and in Europe.

It is believed that letterpress printing from wooden blocks was practised in China some two thousand years ago. Rather strangely, perhaps, it cannot be assumed that people who did letterpress printing would think of applying it to the decoration of fabric. It is a fact that from earliest times, through to the Middle Ages with their rigid guild system, and even today, ideas do not pass easily from trade to trade.

As I have mentioned, it is known that in India during the early part of the Christian era there existed a flourishing textile printing industry and that blocks were used; so the Chinese and the Hindus can both justifiably claim credit for the discovery of block printing.

Rhenish block prints

The beginnings of block printing in Europe are equally hard to trace, but it is believed to have originated in the Middle Ages, and was certainly carried on in several monasteries in the Lower Rhineland district of Germany between the tenth and fourteenth centuries. The fabric used was mainly linen, but some silk examples have been found, all being carried out with surface pigments. There is therefore a strong case for assuming that Germany was responsible for the first block printing in Europe.

It used to be thought that the black printed specimens were the earliest ones and gold and silver was only used in the later work. But a researcher writing in the *CIBA Review* notes that, as the prints were imitating the gold and silver brocades of the period, and were produced by block-printing gum on to the line and then impressing a leaf of metal on to the shape, it is much more likely that the idea of black prints came as a result of observing the effect of the stained gum as the gold or silver leaf became rubbed off.

Briefly, the early designs consist of single or paired animals enclosed in circular shapes; details of tongues etc. are painted in by hand in a fairly bright colour. Later designs discard the containing shape, so giving a more all-over effect. In the fourteenth century figure scenes began to appear with the use of larger blocks.

(*Opposite*) Blockprinted and painted Indian skirt (mid-eighteenth century) typical of those made for the European market.

Rhenish block print in black on natural linen; about thirteenth century.

The cloth (usually linen) was soaked in a solution of parchment scrapings, a by-product of parchment making; this had the effect of stiffening the cloth and making it easier to print. The blocks were usually of walnut or pear-wood. A frame was laid on the table and the cloth to be printed was stretched on this. The square or rectangular block, which was a quarter of the size of the frame, was firmly fixed in one corner of the frame on top of the fabric. Using a small board, the printer rubbed the material against the block from below, and so transferred the pigment colour from it to the cloth. The earliest woodcuts on paper were printed by the same method and indeed a 'cloth-printer' was simply known as a 'printer' until the mid-fifteenth century when the first books were printed.

At first only undyed cloth was patterned, whereas later the colour effects became richer and it was customary to dye the cloth before printing it and often to add extra bits of colour by hand painting or even stencilling. There are a few exceptional examples which display finer lines and which make it fairly certain that sometimes designs were engraved on metal plates – not unlike those used in certain monasteries for printing illuminated manuscripts

England and France

England first saw Indian hand-painted cottons when she raided Portuguese ships, and the impact on the upper classes who could afford to pay the high price asked was, as we have seen, sensational. Greater and greater quantities were demanded until, in 1631, the East India Company was formed and given permission to import them without tax. France reacted in the same way; *toiles peintes*, as they were called, were soon 'high fashion'. It is not difficult to imagine how the people of the time felt: the cottons were light and soft to the touch, delicately coloured and imaginatively patterned, very different from the rich and heavy silks, velvets, brocades and embroidered cloths until then so sought after and admired.

Soon, however, their popularity aroused the anger and concern of the silk and woollen weavers, who began to petition the government of the day to ban the wearing and import of Indian painted 'calicoes' or 'chints'. And in 1700 they achieved their objective. An Act was passed in England forbidding 'calicoes painted, dyed, printed or stained from being worn or otherwise used within the Kingdom.'

In France the desire for Indian goods was, if possible, even greater (partly enhanced by the visit of ambassadors from Siam in 1684), and a ban imposed in 1686 not only forbade the importation of Indian cottons but also tried to stifle interest in even the simple home-produced cottons that had begun to be blockprinted in various places in France itself. Fairs at Saint-Germain and the Val-de-Grâce were ideal places for illegal sales, while in the *enclos privilégiés*, or 'sanctuaries', of various churches, the cloths and the merchants could be safe from law enforcement. It was considered daring and necessary to one's prestige to use as many 'indiennes' as possible for day gowns and as the furnishings for boudoirs and other rooms.

For many years it was believed unquestioningly that as far as England was concerned textile printing was first started at Richmond in 1690, but recent research, in the 1950s, has shown beyond doubt that it was introduced at least fourteen years earlier, possibly by Will Sherwin, who in 1676 set up a works at West Ham 'for the printing of broadcloth'. Studies have been carried out under the late Peter Floud at the Victoria and Albert Museum into early English printed fabrics found in America and elsewhere and proof has been established of the earlier date. By 1690 Will Sherwin's patent had run out and other centres were started at Richmond, Bromley, Crayford, Waltham Abbey, Merton Abbey and several other places. In about 1764 calico printing was started in Lancashire, one of the first printworks being that of Messrs Clayton at Bamber Bridge, near Preston.

Even though at the beginning of the eighteenth century calico printing was largely experimental, involving the use of very simple wood blocks and vegetable dyes, clients soon began to demand high standards. Women were keen connoisseurs of calico printing. Not only had the cloth to look well when new but it had also to wash and wear well; there is an instance recorded of a merchant replacing cloth because it faded after two years. Having a clientèle that could distinguish between good and indifferent workmanship, it was necessary for the producer to take a pride in his work, and printers were considered to be very important people.

One of the great difficulties of the earliest printers lay in not being able to find the right kind of thickenings. No liquid dyestuff will remain in any given shape of its own accord and so to control the shape being printed a thickening agent, usually in the form of a starch or gum, must be added to the mordant (or in modern times to the dye) to facilitate the printing. A certain amount of knowledge of vegetable dyes and the use of mordants, or 'drugs' as they were then called, particularly of madder, woad and indigo and some of the dye-woods, was indeed available even before the detailed revelations passed on by Father Cœurdoux (see also p. 23). But it was a knowledge only of their use in the liquid form, needed for painting. And the Indian and Middle Eastern ability with mordants seems to have been much more thorough than any attempts in Europe before the eighteenth century. In recent years much research has been started into the earliest kinds of thickenings used, because it has at last been realized how vital this aspect is. This research has shown that the early English printers, and also an Irishman, Francis Nixon, who first worked at Drumcondra near Dublin in the 1750s, made great contributions to the fastness and accuracy of calico printing by their experiments.

The earliest prints were simple copies of Indian motifs executed by small wood blocks; but there was also another type of print, which was fine, detailed and one-colour printed from engraved copper plates. Bans on home-produced goods were not enforced in England until 1720, but in 1719 it was written in a political pamphlet: 'in spite of the import ban . . . the first class were clothed in the outlawed Indian Chints, the second with English and Dutch printed cottons and the rest in plain "calicoes" – all this instead of English and Venetian brocades and silk damasks or even plain worsteds.' The position became so bad that rioting broke out when mobs of weavers and their supporters attacked women wearing printed cottons.

However, after several years of largely unsuccessful attempts to enforce a total ban on fabric printing in both France and England, restrictions were gradually lifted, first to allow printing on fustian – a fabric with a linen warp and cotton weft – and finally to give complete freedom, in France in 1759 and five years later in England too. It has been suggested that, particularly in France, some of the bans were brought about not simply to satisfy the jealous vested interests of the established industries, but because it was felt that the standards of blockmaking and printing, and certainly of dye fastness, were not good enough to allow it to continue unchecked. And it is a fact that the government inspectors of dyehouses reacted favourably to the better standards of the late 1750s and the ban was lifted immediately afterwards. In the light of recent research, it is thought possible that the use of unsatisfactory thickeners may well have been another contributory factor to the dissatisfaction.

Within four years of the final lifting of restrictions in England the $3\frac{1}{2}d.$ per yard tax paid by printers of cottons was refunded on goods exported, and Oberkamphe, the great French textile printer, was also doing a great trade with several countries. Although printing did continue illicitly during the bans, on a variety of mixed cloths, obviously the restrictions hampered experiments and held back the industry. Those areas of France around Mulhouse, which were part of the Swiss commune at the time of the restrictions, were able to forge ahead. There are still firms there that were founded at the time of the prohibition, and from that time it has always been an area famous for technical achievements in textile production.

BLOCKMAKING

Before describing in detail the various methods by which blocks were made in the eighteenth century it is important to realize that these same methods are used today by the few firms in England and Europe who still carry on block printing as a means of producing exclusive fabrics for a specialized market. Blocks cut from wood, infilled with felt and where necessary incorporating copper strip, continue to be made and used today, but from the mid-nineteenth century onwards cast metal blocks, which are cheaper to produce, have on the whole taken over for designs with small repeats. The first results from cast or stereo blocks were poor, but by the early 1900s these almost entirely superseded those made from copper or brass strips and pins. At present few craftsmen remain who are skilled in 'coppering', as it was called; in any case, it is too slow a method to be economic even in the highly priced market occupied by blockprinted fabrics. However, David Evans Ltd of Crayford in Kent, one of the oldest-established printworks in the country, still make their own wood and cast blocks and are finding that there is an increasing interest in the various blockmaking methods, particularly in America and Japan. The few small firms who are still block printing mostly get their new blocks, on the rare occasions when these are needed, from a small village in Austria, where the craft is still practised. For all blocks, fairly hard woods are used, such as ash, box, lime, sycamore, holly, and particularly pearwood. (Nowadays African hardwoods are often used.) Several thicknesses are glued together with the grain running in different directions.

The *simple wood block* was used exclusively in the early and mid-eighteenth century for any line work and also for shapes that were not too big. In fact areas over $\frac{1}{8}$–$\frac{1}{4}$ in. in width do

not print well because the wood does not hold the water-based dyes evenly enough to give a regular result. To transfer a line drawing on to a simple wood block, the blockmaker makes an outline tracing of the design with a mixture of lampblack and linseed oil on transparent paper. He lays this face downwards on the smooth surface of the wood and burnishes it to transfer the lines. The parts to be reserved are then tinted with a watercolour (often pink). After this, the block cutter uses a chisel to cut away the background and the insides of the parts that are not required to print, to a

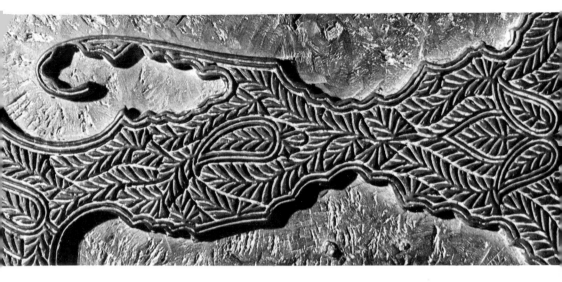

depth of $\frac{1}{4}$–$\frac{3}{4}$ in. according to the type of shape and the fabric that is to be printed on (fine cloth needing less deep cutting).

When bigger areas of colour are to be printed, a *colour block* is used. To make this, the craftsmen begin by tracing the outline of the design on to the block as before. Next, the wood is cut into, to within about $\frac{1}{16}$–$\frac{1}{8}$ in. inside the traced outline of the shape, and then removed to a depth of $\frac{1}{4}$ in. or so, leaving a narrow wall of wood. Thick felt, which has been soaked in water and gum, is pressed partly into the hollowed-out shape to outline it on the felt. Then this shape is cut out in felt and pressed into the centre of the motif so that it is level with the wooden outline. The wood outside the shape is then carved away, leaving a firm area of pattern in felt with a supporting wall of wood. It is easy to see how fairly large forms can be well printed by this means, because the felt holds the dye readily and allows the block to give up its colour evenly to the cloth.

In the latter half of the eighteenth century, fine pieces of brass or copper in the form of strips or 'pins' began to be added to the wood blocks, to enable more intricate details to be rendered. It was this type of innovation that very quickly made an impact on design styles and 'pinning', or *picotage* as the French called it, was used in many ways. Shadowy patterns are printed from areas made up entirely of pins, or pinned details form part of the design. Sometimes, before printing the pattern, the whole cloth was over-printed with a fine pin-spot ground known as 'vermicular', or in France *sablé* (sanded) ground. This only showed faintly through the flowers and leaves, and gave a pleasingly dainty effect to the rest of the cloth.

Later, in the nineteenth century, detail and line blocks were made entirely of metal strips (brass or copper) hammered into the wooden base and were known as *coppered blocks*. The metal was first made to the right size and cross-

Two wood blocks which, although not from the eighteenth century, illustrate the kind of detail that can be achieved: (*opposite*) an early nineteenth-century example whose simple shapes are made interesting and printable by means of the gouged-out linear details; (*above*) a fairly recent block from the Lebanon, remarkable for the intricacy of its fern-like pattern.

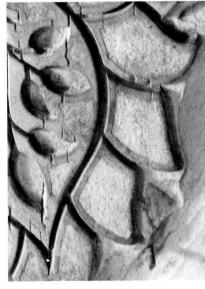

A detail from a William Morris 'bleach' or discharge block, showing the support walls of wood with felt infilling necessary for printing large even areas.

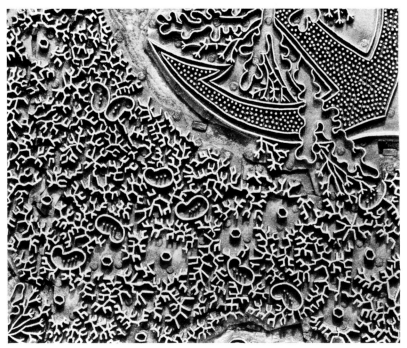

(*Above, right*) A 'pinned' stripe or border block, dated about 1880.

(*Above*) A late nineteenth-century block showing 'pinning' and a seaweed pattern which became rather popular, and which obviously grew out of the 'coppering' method.

(*Opposite*) Eighteenth-century French cotton – a superb example of the use of 'pins' to produce a highly decorative background pattern. (This should not be confused with the 'vermicular' or 'sablé' style, where the whole cloth was printed over very finely, and then the main flower or other pattern was printed on top.)

section by drawing it through a plate with holes in it of the desired shape and size. After tracing the design on to the surface of the wood, the block cutter chisels away the outline of the shape – *not* the ground as before – to a depth of about $\frac{1}{4}$ in. The strips of copper or brass are then driven into the groove. (A piece of metal of the required depth is used as a gauge beside the copper, or brass, so that the blockmaker knows how deep to drive it in.) By this means, spots or lines of widths varying from $\frac{1}{64}$ to $\frac{1}{16}$ in. can be obtained fairly easily and are of ample strength to withstand the hard wear of printing for years. Also, many other forms such as ovals, rings, diamonds, stars or rosettes can be produced from rods of similar-sized section.

Since these coppered blocks nearly always have to be handled by the printer manually, they must not be too big or too heavy: no more than 10 lb. in weight and no larger than $18 \times 18 \times 2\frac{1}{2}$ in. In the eighteenth and nineteenth centuries, most blocks were much smaller than this and, as recorded in the *British Manufacturers Companion* of 1791, it follows that many blocks were used in designs with, say, only six or eight colours, because there had to be several made for each colour. By no means always square or rectangular, they were often quite irregular in shape, because all spare wood had been cut away.

Only three other things need to be done before the block is ready for use. The wood is given a coating of waterproof varnish to preserve it for as long as possible. Then two finger-grip holes are made in the back of the block to enable the printer to pick it up easily and hold it securely.

Making wood blocks at David Evans Printworks, Crayford, Kent.

Finally, brass pins are driven in at the corners for registration purposes, to ensure accurate repeating of patterns. These are known as 'pitch pins' and their use will be fully explained on p. 39. The making of good pitch pins is important because they can so easily cause a badly fitting pattern and ruin a piece of cloth. Even if you exercise extreme care, registration can be difficult and joins have to be concealed by the skilful placing of leaves and other motifs. In late Georgian times there was a fashion for dark plum or even black grounds, and where this was to occur the cutter left a thick edge of black on the outside of his outline. Known as 'boundage', this helped the printer to fit each colour accurately.

When one thinks that every line and shape drawn by the designer has to be translated into either wood or metal, it becomes easier to appreciate the great skill and sensitivity displayed by the craftsmen (particularly in the eighteenth and nineteenth centuries). Not only do they need to be skilful with tools but they must have a feeling for the qualities of the design they are interpreting; and this sensitivity and skill continued to give block prints their notable excellence of reproduction which lasted even when the machine age began to bring about a change in standards.

PRINTING WITH HAND BLOCKS

The construction and size of table used for block printing and the means of transferring the colour to the block are entirely traditional. This fact can be seen clearly by comparing illustrations of block printing in the early nineteenth century with those at William Morris's Merton Abbey printworks, in about 1885, and with the photographs of printing at David Evans of Crayford today. It is still the custom to have short tables of only $8\frac{1}{2}$ to 10 yards in length.

The table must be very firm, stable and strong, with a top that is able to withstand the blows from the printer's mallet without movement or becoming untrue. It must therefore have a metal or thick slate top, covered – as all printing surfaces must be – with a woollen blanket to give resilience and a waterproof topping to prevent the blanket from becoming soiled. A firm yet resilient table-covering is essential for all types of fabric printing, whether block, engraved roller or screen, and the high quality of the blanket (and continual checking and replacement) is one of the costlier aspects of the job. Over the waterproof topping stretch a length of plain, smooth cotton, known in all printworks as a 'back-grey'. The function of the back-grey is to absorb any colour which penetrates to the underside of the cloth and which, if allowed to touch the non-absorbent waterproof skin, would spread out to give a blurred print. The back-grey may be gummed to the waterproof topping or simply stretched tightly over it before the fabric to be printed is laid on top. When printing a short length, the size of the table, the fabric can be pinned to the back-grey along the selvedge at about three-inch intervals. Alternatively, the printer fixes a roll of cloth at one end of the table, just above floor level, and then draws off sufficient yardage to cover the table and pins that in position. After printing, he draws the cloth off the table on to another roller above the far end of the table (at ceiling height). He does not wind the cloth round this wooden roller until it is dry.

Since the earliest days of block printing in Europe the device used to hold the printing colour, suitably thickened for printing, has been known as a 'swimming-tub', or sometimes as a 'sieve'. Just as it is essential to have a resilient surface on the table to make a good print, so is the presentation of the colour from a springy pad important to enable the printer to get the colour on to the surface of the block evenly. The swimming-tub consists of a wooden tub about 20–22 inches square almost filled with old colour or a starchy thickening, simply to give resilience. On top of this, a slightly smaller drum stretched over with waterproof cloth is inverted, resting on the thickening. Then over this again is stretched a fine, evenly woven piece of woollen cloth. The object of the tub is to ensure as even as possible a distribution of colour on to the block, rather as an ink-pad is used to ink a rubber stamp.

Printing the border on a Liberty silk scarf. Notice that the printer is positioning the block by means of the pitch pins on the two corners nearest to him, and also that with such a small block on fine silk he does not need a wooden mallet or maul.

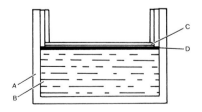

Diagrammatic section of the 'swimming-tub': A wooden tub; B thickening or old dye-paste; C drum stretched with a waterproof covering; D drum stretched with a piece of fine woollen cloth on which the dye-paste being used is spread with a brush.

Early nineteenth-century block printing, from *Practical Handbook of Dyeing and Calico-printing*, published in 1874 by W. Crookes.

Block printing at David Evans Printworks, Crayford, Kent.

Block printing in the nineteenth century: blocks successively applied to produce the different shades in a flower. From the *Practical Handbook of Dyeing and Calico-printing*.

The printer employs an assistant, who brushes the printing colour evenly over the stretched woollen cloth of the sieve. (This task is known as 'tearing' or 'tiering' and the women or boys who did the job were called 'tearers'.) The printer then presses the block on to the sieve in two opposite directions to ensure an even coating of colour on the printing surface. It is obvious from this that the correct tension of the piece of woollen cloth is vitally important: if it is left too slack the colour may be transferred accidentally to the vertical walls of the pattern shapes. The necessity of keeping the colour on the top printing surface only is also the reason for not brushing directly on to the block.

Next comes the 'registering' of the blocks, or the establishing of their correct placing on the cloth. As we have seen, the blockmaker has inserted pitch pins in each corner of the block, to be used by the printer to ensure correct and accurate register in printing. Each pin prints a small, precise dot, and as printing continues the pins at the head of the rectangle determine the position for the next placement of the base pins. Sideways register for lateral movement across the cloth is similarly determined by previous impressions. For larger patterns in which more than one block is needed to complete a repeat, each block will have pitch pins to determine the positioning of the next block vertically or horizontally.

When the block is in position on the cloth, the printer takes an iron-headed mallet, or printer's 'maul', and resting its head on the heel of his hand he strikes the back of the block a couple of times with the end of the wooden handle. The mallet is used in this way in order to spread the weight

Part of the border of an Italian *mezzaro* – a large shawl worn by peasant women, which covered the head and shoulders and hung down to the ground. The main centre for the production of these *mezzari* was Genoa from about 1787 to 1848. The Swiss craftsmen Giovanni and Michel Speich and Luigi Testori used as many as eighty blocks to build up large 'Tree of Life' patterns after the Indian style. This photograph shows how blocks were skilfully shaped to create tonal effects within the flowers.

from the blows evenly over the surface, thereby giving an even print. If the head were used it would be a more confined blow which might lead to a spotty and irregular impression. The tearer brushes the colour over the sieve again, the printer recharges the block with colour, uses the printed pitch marks to register the block in the second position as previously described, and printing carries on until completed. A second colour is positioned by pins or tiny pattern shapes which can be 'pitched' on already printed shapes. Sometimes the required depth of colour can be attained by simply pressing the block on to the cloth, instead of using the mallet, for instance if the block is small and very light in weight and the cloth fine and thin.

THE EIGHTEENTH CENTURY

To return to block printing in the eighteenth century, it is plain to see that the insistence on care and quality did not come from the customer alone; among many printers there was a tremendous urge to improve their technique and a keen desire for new knowledge. Take, for example, the repeated requests for detailed information about Indian madder dyeing methods made to Father Cœurdoux, the French trading missionary, by a contact in France.

In the *British Manufacturers Companion and Callico Printers Assistant*, by Charles O'Brien, written in 1791 (and possibly the first book of its kind), the author comments:

> a query, which might with propriety have been put to the Printer, which is, If he had been printing that piece as a present for a favourite female, whether he would not have bestowed a little more consideration on the particular alluded to [the repeat].

This treatise gives minutely detailed rules and guidelines intended to help all the different people who contributed to the production of a piece of blockprinted cloth, and which still help us today; on designers:

> In the first place, it is suggested, a Designer ought not, by any means, to be considered in so mechanical a light, as if fancy or invention were of such a nature, that he can at all times command a successful operation; [here is meant an engaged designer who works a stated number of hours a day] similar to a person performing a merely mechanical piece of work. Designers should only work when so disposed, yet many think nothing done unless they see something on paper; making hardly any account of what the invention is at work upon.

The designer 'should have a knowledge of the business in every stage of its process', and:

> In drawing trail patterns, . . . flowers and other objects . . . first mark their distance, observing to make the trail spread regularly . . . keeping two or more objects that are similar in shape and colour, as far from each other as you can.

On 'putting on' (i.e. transferring the design to the surface of the block) the instructions are:

> In drawing leaves . . . that are to be pencilled, [i.e. put in by hand] it is recommended to terminate them as fig. 26 27 or fig. 28, as such a finish will keep the penciling, particularly the blue colour, on account of its thickness, from being run into the white,

and on 'pitches':

> At the head the pitches should stand out from the work near one quarter of an inch, that the wood may not press on the cloth . . . put stout pieces of wire deep in the wood, rather slanting, and lessen the tops with a file . . .
>
> To be more certain of having your pitch pins in their proper places, they had better be put in before prints or grounds are cut . . .

Blocks should not be 'above nine inches long, it being handier for working and not so apt to warp . . . and for very close fine prints that are difficult to join, the smaller they are

THE

BRITISH *Manufacturers Companion*,

AND

CALLICO PRINTERS ASSISTANT;

BEING A

TREATISE *on* CALLICO PRINTING,

In all its Branches, Theoretical and Practical;

WITH AN

ESSAY *on Genius, Invention, and Designing;*

RULES FOR

Drawing, Cutting, Printing, Engraving, Co-
lour-making, Bleaching, &c.

Suggeftions for the Advantage of Manufactures;
And many valuable Hints to the Proprietors of Print-fields.

BY CHARLES OBRIEN, *Callico Printer.*

LONDON:

PRINTED FOR THE AUTHOR;

AND SOLD BY HAMILTON AND CO. AT THE
BUST OF SHAKSPEARE, BEECH-STREET,
NEAR FINSBURY-SQUARE; AND
VERNOR AND HOOD, BIRCHIN-LANE, CORNHILL.

The frontispiece of *The British
Manufacturers Companion and
Callico Printers Assistant* by Charles
O'Brien, 1791. This was the first
book of its kind in England.

the better', and on the use and management of blocks, the
author says:

> Blocks should be kept in a rather dry place, without a
> fire, at a convenient distance from the ground; those
> intended for prints seen to require laying with their faces
> downwards, and those for grounds with their faces
> upwards.

On 'squaring' a block he advises:

> have a plate of copper or pewter, set out with a number
> of squares within each other, of the different sizes . . .
> [repeats, that is] and set into as many divisions as you
> chuse and at the corners of each square, and wherever the
> divisions are marked let there be holes pierced through, as

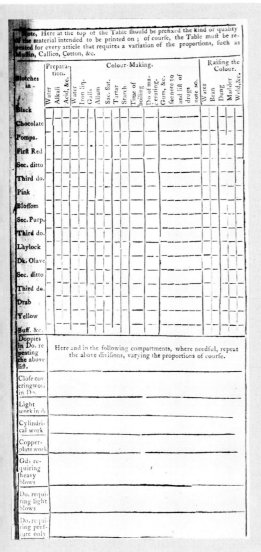

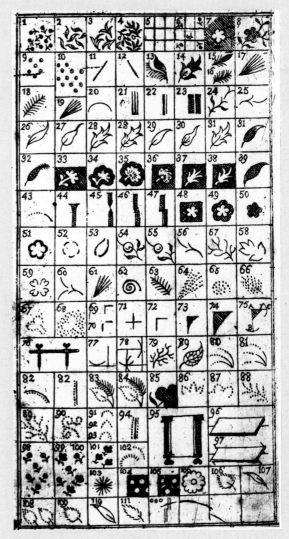

fine and strait as possible; you have then only to lay your plate on a block or paper, and with a fine needle prick through the holes . . . and then rule as usual from the pricked holes left on.

Another method is by having a piece of thin wood or metal, made angular as fig. 74, which laying on a block or paper, rule two lines [as] fig. 75.

Instructions for pinning are:

The quicker pins are put in, the firmer they hold; and the more uniformly upright they are put in, the evener they work; for if put in very slanting, the setting of them upright afterwards, loosens them at the bottom . . . If you have a flower, or leaf . . . as fig. 86, begin at the points, and

(*Above, left*) An early form of work-sheet, and (*above*) a page of diagrams, both from the *Manufacturers Companion*. It is interesting to note the different methods of impressing the blocks on to the cloth, for example with 'heavy blows'.

then fill up the line as regularly as you can . . . A first impression of every print, and the last joined one, with the grounds, should be carefully preserved;

and for the preparation of the cloth:

> good printing depends a great deal on the manner in which the cloth is got up; but particularly, how it is calendered.
>
> When a printer takes a new print in hand, his first care is to try on paper, or a trial piece, that it is in the square, the pitches firm in their places, that the print does not want mending . . . good printing cannot be performed without good tearing, [i.e. spreading on of colour on the woollen sieve]; and good tearing can only be such, when a proper and equal quantity of colour is disposed over the sieve.

With such detailed instructions to help them it is small wonder that the blocks were so well cut and the printed cottons so delightful.

It is interesting to see how well the blockmakers interpreted flower drawings and designs and how the various methods of making them and the materials used had a definite influence on the development of design styles. In both England and France, as well as Portugal and Holland, designs progressed from being poor copies of Indian flowers and 'pinecones' and soon began to develop into the delicate sprigs, sprays and cabbage roses so characteristic of English fabrics, and the 'fleurettes', ribbons and stripes, and 'bonnes herbes' traditional in France.

An interesting point for designers to note is that even then France was undoubtedly recognized to be the leader in designing and producing fabrics. A reason is given in the final extract from the *Manufacturers Companion*:

> as merely practical men in extensive businesses are more alive to immediate 'Loss and Gain', than to distant advantages, which require deviations from established modes of practice or supplies, the greatest discoveries sometimes produce only a transient blaze, and are, alas! consigned to oblivion.

In France, at Jouy-en-Josas on the river Bièvre, near Versailles, well-known artists and flower-painters such as Mlle Jouanon and 'Peter' were employed in creating designs; but the important point, according to O'Brien, is that it was in Jouy that the new practical developments kept up with the new design ideas, and the working of the two together made certain of keeping the Manufacture de Jouy very much in the lead. The owner of the factory, Christophe-Philippe Oberkamphe, enjoyed Royal patronage and the author suggests that 'a premium from a Royal source', paid as an inducement in the developing of practical ideas, would give English artists sufficient incentive to emulate French ones.

Artists such as one referred to as 'Mr Edwards FSA' [Fellow of the Royal Society of Arts] painted flowers as patterns for Queen Caroline's furniture, but the type of design, although highly desirable, was too intricate for calico printing – at least at the price per yard the printer could hope to charge. So the conclusion was: 'until these things are remedied English Callico-printing will ever be behind that of the Continent, especially what is now [1791] attempting at Jouy, near Versailles in France.'

A woven Paisley shawl with a white ground, dated between 1820 and 1845.

MECHANIZATION OF BLOCK PRINTING

Because block printing was popular but was tending to lose ground as a result of the much faster cylinder printing, there were many attempts to mechanize it and so enable it to compete for price with the new method (see p. 67). But some extremely good hand block printing continued up to about 1860, when it virtually disappeared altogether until William Morris revived the method in the 1870s. Since then it has continued for the production of very expensive silk and fine wools – particularly for discharge work – until the present day, although in 1967 even Liberty's closed their blockprinting department.

In about 1840 printed versions of the popular Paisley shawls began to appear. The true woven Paisley shawls were modelled on the style of the ones from Kashmir made from

A close-up of the centre of the shawl on page 45, illustrating the type of detail copied in many Victorian blockprinted woollen cloths as well as in the shawls themselves.

a fine quality of goat's wool. Already by 1790 at least three places in Europe had been trying to copy them – Lyons, Norwich and Edinburgh. But, labour being very cheap in Paisley, the bulk of the weaving industry began to shift there. The 'pinecone' motif appeared in shawls in about 1816, but by about 1840 the designs were nearly all of this type. It was impossible to emulate the fine softness, yet strength, of the Kashmir fabric with British wool and so often silk warps, or a reinforcement of silk, was needed. After about 1840 Jacquard looms were used and enabled greater freedom of pattern than the old drawloom.

The earliest printed shawls were on very fine silk and the standard of blockmaking and printing was extremely high. Later, wool and cotton were printed on. The best blocks used for the purpose were the intricately constructed coppered ones, although both wood and also cast ones were used. The blockmakers displayed amazing skill and ingenuity in the way they adapted their craft of cutting and hammering small strips of copper or brass into the wooden

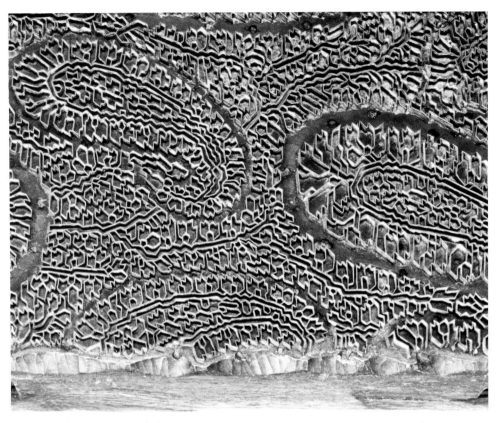

Two 'coppered' blocks of the type used to print Paisley shawl patterns.

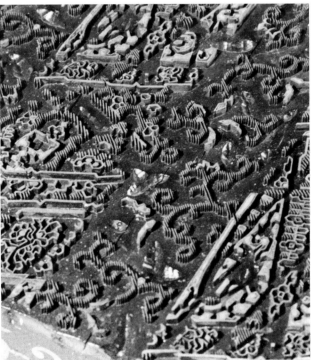

block, in imitation of the broken weave effects which were a characteristic of the originals. The printed imitations were indistinguishable from the woven ones a few feet away. Printing was, of course, a means of producing a cheaper article, but even so, great care and taste for colour was evident in the making of the printed materials, and block printing in Victorian times attained and maintained very high standards indeed. It did not seem to be affected by the lowered standards of some of the other printing methods.

The surface roller machine

The first development in the mechanization of block printing was the surface roller machine, invented by a Frenchman, Ebinger, in 1800; it was really intended to imitate Bell's cylinder machine (see p. 67). Although he was successful in

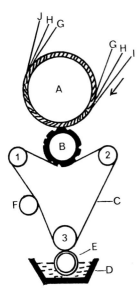

Diagram of surface roller printing machine: A pressure bowl; B surface roller; C furnishing blanket moving over rollers 1, 2 and 3; D colour trough; E plain furnishing roller rotating in colour; F second furnishing roller spreading colour evenly on the blanket; G blanket for extra resilience round the pressure bowl; H back-grey; I cloth to be printed; J printed cloth.

(*Left*) A printed Paisley of about 1845.

A twentieth-century Sanderson furnishing fabric showing the characteristics of the surface roller printing method.

creating a continuous printing machine, it was not very workable. The wooden rollers warped and split very quickly and the transference of the colour was rather unsatisfactory and caused the prints to be inferior in every way to flat block work.

Shortly afterwards a man named Burch, of Church, near Blackburn in Lancashire, successfully experimented with surface roller (or continuous relief) printing. The rollers were coppered and felted in the manner described for flat blocks and then the lower surfaces were well varnished. The colour was furnished from an endless blanket on which it had been evenly spread by two plain rollers – one rotating in the colour trough and the other distributing it. On leaving the furnishing roller the sieve was wiped by a steel 'doctor' blade (see p. 70). In 1805, Burch also developed a 'union' or 'mule' machine combining in one machine an engraved copper cylinder with a wooden roller in relief.

Surface roller printing is still carried on a little for traditional chintz designs, for example at Sandersons, but its main development is in the field of wallpaper printing. It is a fairly difficult machine to operate and so its use has tended to diminish in the twentieth century. Prints executed by this means often exhibit a 'squashed-out' effect due to the rounded surface of the cylindrical block.

The Perrotine

In 1834 Perrot of Rouen invented a mechanical block-printing machine, the Perrotine. This machine mechanically performed all the actions of the blockprinter, that is it put colour on the sieves, transferred it to the blocks, stamped the blocks on the cloth and then moved the cloth forward after each repeat.

The Perrotine was obviously regarded with great favour at the time, for within two years of its invention it is believed that about sixty machines were sold in Europe. The Perrotine was never popular in England, but elsewhere it superseded hand blockprinting to a great extent. One obvious reason for the comparative lack of interest in the machine in Great Britain was the fact that by the late 1830s Bell's cylinder machine had gained so much ground and indeed at the beginning of the nineteenth century England had plunged so eagerly into mass production that the blockprinting machine was not sufficiently speedy.

However, as well as largely preserving the hand-block character of the printing (for the small-scale and repetitive type of work it could do) the Perrotine had a number of other advantages. For one, the whole width of the cloth was printed at the same time, which ensured a certain regularity of repeat. Moreover, not only did it increase production 250 per cent, but there was a better registration of colours. The main disadvantage was that repeats of more than $5\frac{1}{2}$ inches in height were not possible.

(*Opposite*) Blockprinted wall-hanging from Masulipatam, India (eighteenth century).

In very simplified terms, the Perrotine machine consists of five main parts: cast-iron tables; sieves; mechanical tearers (comprising a brush and colour-box); a block carrier, which operated so subtly that it managed to copy the action of a hand blockprinter; and, finally, an arrangement for drawing the cloth forward after printing. The three wooden blocks about 30 inches long by $2-5\frac{1}{2}$ inches broad are fixed with the pattern sides at right angles to each other in a strong iron frame. They can each in turn be brought down on to the front, top and back of a four-sided 'table' covered with cloth and revolving on an axis. The cloth to be printed passes between the table and the blocks and gets its pattern in succession. The blocks are forced down upon the calico by means of springs with a complicated mechanism which cleverly copies the type of pressure given by a hand block-printer.

After each printing the block is recharged with colour from a flannel (the sieve), which has had colour applied evenly by a mechanically operated brush. The sieves are flat, and work in grooves on the sides of the tables, receiving colour from the furnishing rollers which they then pass on to the blocks. Another ingenious idea is the one used to regulate the amount of dye-paste put on the block. The rollers are fitted with levers which can be made to exert greater or less pressure in order to control the quantity of colour applied. As the cloth passes round the three sides of the cast-iron table it is held in position at the corners and prevented from slipping by rollers whose surfaces are covered with needle-points. The machine could be operated by hand with a winch or by steam power.

In his *Practical Handbook of Dyeing & Calico-printing*, published in 1874, W. Crookes gives a very detailed description of the Perrotine in motion:

> The piece moves on a length equal to the breadth of the pattern-blocks, along with the blanket and back-cloth. The portion of the piece which issues from the third block is fully printed; what was under the second advances under the third; what was under the first moves to the second, whilst a fresh portion of white calico comes up to the first. While the calico is moving the sieves take up position and all three press on the furnishing rollers, taking up the colour spread evenly there by the brushes. Then the sliding block-holders move forward, and push the blocks against the sieves, so furnishing them with colour. At the same time the slides give the blocks a gentle movement backwards, while the sieves deviate from their position. On returning the blocks, having been pressed against a fresh part of the colour surface, are drawn back again, prior to printing that part of the calico next in position; the cycle then continues.

The Perrotine was still in use in Germany as late as 1946 for the West Africa printing trade.

(Opposite) The blockprinted *Snake-head* chintz by William Morris, 1876.

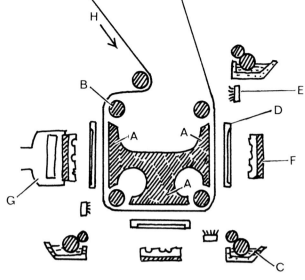

Diagrammatic section of the Perrotine machine: A cast-iron tables; B guide rollers; C colour-boxes and furnishing roller; D sieves; E brushes; F printing blocks, usually 30 in. long by 3 to $5\frac{1}{4}$ in. wide; G block carriers.

A Perrotine machine.

CAST OR STEREOTYPE BLOCKS

In about 1850 a new way of making blocks was developed, and cast or stereotype blocks were evolved. Although this cast method caused some deterioration in quality of line and detail, it can now be done with skill, and good cast blocks are to be found. The first ones, very crudely made, were produced in France in 1842, but after various experiments the results by 1850 were much better; they were used widely in the Perrotine. This same method is used today almost exclusively for the production of fine line and detail blocks – the ones for instance which print small tie-silk designs and tiny Paisleys, particularly for discharge work. Although one cannot expect the subtle variations of line that are possible from a coppered or finely cut wood block, a careful craftsman can produce surprisingly good prints. The best wood for making the mould is probably old, seasoned lime, but, as with simple wood blocks, African hardwoods are often used now.

To make the mould, one repeat (or several, according to the size of the design) is traced with carbon paper on to the smoothed and polished end of the grain of a suitable piece of wood by the blockmaker; this wood will be a few inches bigger than the area of the design used. Then the block-maker burns the pattern into the wood with a small, specially made brass tool. The craftsman's skill lies in the

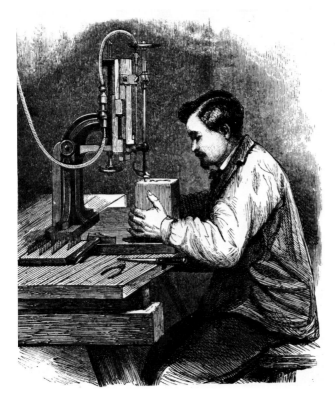

An early illustration of mould-making for cast blocks, using a gas-heated device (*Practical Handbook of Dyeing and Calico-printing*).

Typical Victorian patterns made in cast blocks (*Practical Handbook of Dyeing and Calico-printing*).

making of these tools, one of which has to be made for every separate shape in the design. Usually each block-maker makes his own sets of tools. They are cut out of solid brass and can be amazingly intricate and delicate.

He then fits a tool on to a rod which is gas- or electrically heated; it was originally preheated and later always gas-heated. This tool has a gauge on it so that the wood will be burned only to the required depth. To one side of the pattern area he cuts a groove and slopes away the area above the pattern. Then he presses a piece of metal up against the groove, making with the sloped-away wood a small trough into which the type metal can be poured by an assistant.

Many of these casts are made, to form the necessary number of repeats. The casts are then riveted to the laminated block of wood which has been already prepared. By tradition, not necessity, the top surface of this block is still very often pearwood. Finally, the blockmaker polishes the top surface of the metal and makes it level, smooth and so ready for use.

Some fairly large and not very detailed blocks, for use on work such as African prints, are still made out of wood and felt, and are routed out by small electrically heated routing machines instead of by hand chiselling (like the traditional simple wood block). In the mid-nineteenth century also there were two other adaptations to blockprinting techniques which are worthy of mention – although neither is used today. These were: 'tobying', a means of printing several colours at once from one block provided that they were in isolation from each other in the design, and 'fondu', or rainbowing, which was used for shading several colours together.

Toby printing

If several colours were detached from each other the shapes could be all cut into the one block and printed at the same

Two cast blocks illustrating the way in which the separate casts or stereos were fitted together to make (*left*) an all-over pattern, and (*above*) a border.

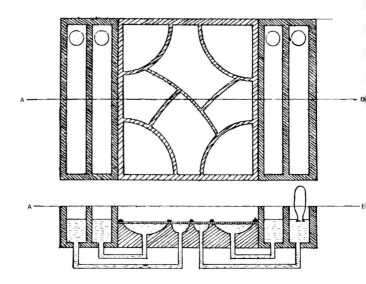

Tobying sieve, showing the divisions. The colours are supplied to the compartments by pipes.

time by means of a divided or 'tobying' sieve. A fine woollen cloth was cemented to the tops of the walls which divided up the specially constructed box for holding the colour. This ensured that when the block was pressed on to the sieve it would receive only a particular colour in each section, supplied to the sieve by connecting tubes from below. The tubes were connected in turn to colour-boxes at the sides. Toby printing was obviously impossible in conjunction with the Perrotine machine.

Rainbowing or 'fondu'

This method of inducing the colours to melt gradually into each other was on the other hand often used to add interest to the small repeat designs printed by Perrotine. The only deviation from normal block printing was in the way the sieve was furnished with colour. This was accomplished by a special colour-lifter which dropped small pools of the various colours on to the sieve, and these were then spread length-wise into overlapping stripes with a piece of wood or a roller. Fondu has not been used for many years but it was the means of producing many beautiful and unusual effects in the early and mid-Victorian times; the year 1850 was one in which the method was extremely fashionable and many fabrics were produced in this way.

A nineteenth-century American bridal quilt, mainly in red, blue, yellow and green interestingly shaded cottons. The quilt is in the possession of the American Museum, Bath.

(*Below, left*) A detail of the quilt, showing the rainbowing effect.

(*Below, right*) Rainbowing equipment, showing the colour lifter which dropped pools of different colours on to the sieve, and the spreader.

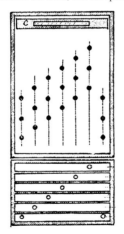

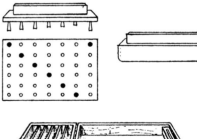

3 Copper-plate printing

Whereas in block printing the cloth receives its pattern from the surface of the block (as in letterpress printing), in copper-plate printing colour is held in the incised lines and the pattern is transferred from them to the cloth by pressure. This is known as an 'intaglio' process. Copper-plate prints of a sort had been done on cloth, mainly silk, during the seventeenth century. Such items as maps, religious broadsheets, and certificates and also embroidery patterns were printed in this way, but these were all in inks that were not washable. The development, already mentioned, by Nixon in the 1750s of a suitable thickening for the mordants made it possible to use the madder dyes and so print fast, washable colours. The thickener obviously had to be of a different type and viscosity from those being used for block printing, because of the finer and more detailed line work which could be engraved on the copper. Apart from the extremely fine line drawing, tonal effects and much larger repeats were the immediate outcome of plate printing. It was a lengthy and expensive process to engrave a design, but from one plate a piece of fabric 1 yard square could be printed at one time.

The earliest dated copper-plate printed fabrics are inscribed 'R. Jones 1761 Old Ford'; the subject consists of classical ruins and hunting scenes. Another one is stamped with the name 'Collins Woolmer'. Plate prints were single-colour designs in blue, purple, and crimson, although one rare specimen has extra colours added by wood blocks afterwards. It is fairly certain that this type of printing was first applied to cloth in Ireland, for there was definitely a textile industry there as early as 1719. Nixon is considered to be the printer who first succeeded in producing fast colours on cloth while retaining the sharpness and clarity of impression so characteristic of copper-plate engraving. In 1754, after working for about two years, he allowed his secret to be sent to London, probably because he planned to move there himself; he did so between 1755 and 1757 and the Irish printworks closed down.

By good fortune our knowledge of English plate prints of the mid-eighteenth century was greatly broadened by the finding in the 1950s of a large number of prints on paper at Mulhouse in France. These were customers' samples, often carried out in this manner. Among them there were about forty furnishing fabric designs and some smaller ones for

(*Opposite*) English plate-printed fabric by Nixon & Co. at Phippsbridge, near Merton, London, 1770.

English copper-plate print *Large Flowers* by Talwin and Foster, printed at Bromley Hall, 1765–75. This is a print in purple on paper, as customers' samples often were, and was among those found at Mulhouse in 1955. The whole large repeat was engraved on one plate and the undulating white background shapes were used skilfully to conceal the fact that there is no join.

dress goods. Floral designs, often of exotic plants as well as ones of English country flowers, were by far the biggest group found there. Sometimes birds were introduced amongst the foliage, the inspiration often coming from the botanical or bird books of the period. In fact it is usual to find the same prints used on transfer-printed enamel and ceramic wares. Because the copper plate could be so big, these large florals (or other designs) had the whole repeat engraved on the one plate – this repeat being very well disguised. But even so it is just possible to trace an undulating white space which runs horizontally across the plates, thus eliminating the need for a difficult join. A number of the florals found at Mulhouse were printed at Bromley Hall by Talwin and Foster from 1765 to 1775. Apart from florals and bird prints there were pastoral and classical designs, the latter a fashion inspired by the excavations at Pompeii and Herculaneum.

Many of the finest and best prints of this type come from France. In 1759, the year that restrictions on printing were finally and completely lifted, Oberkamphe opened his factory at Jouy (see p. 44). Although he produced many glorious designs of different types, it is the single-colour 'island' patterns printed from finely engraved copper plates that spring to mind immediately his name is mentioned. Indeed, if you were to go into a high-class interior decorators in London or Paris and ask for a 'toile de Jouy' you would almost certainly be offered a modern, roller-printed version of this type of cloth.

THE PLATE PRESS

As well as the problem of a correct colour thickening, another difficulty in this type of printing lay in the rather unsatisfactory kind of flat press in use at the time. It was

Toile de Jouy *Travaux de la Manufacture*, the first design by the famous designer Jean-Baptiste Huet for the Oberkamphe factory.

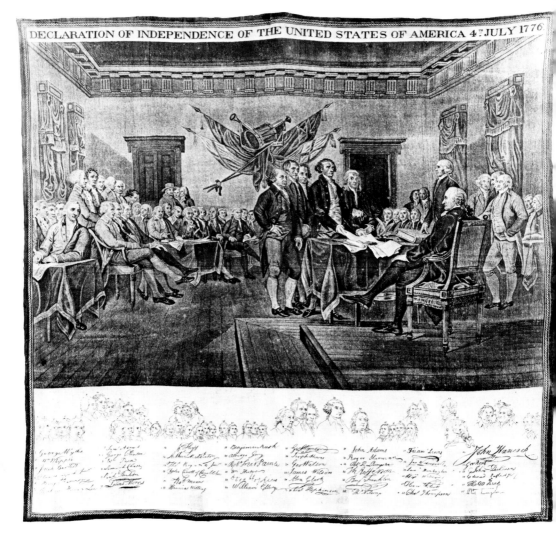

During the latter half of the eighteenth century, many plate-printed squares of a commemorative nature were exported to America from printworks in England and Scotland. The photograph shows a print of the Declaration of Independence in 1776, with signatures of all the participants at the ceremony.

awkward to print anything on it except very small pieces of fabric. However, in about 1770, an improved press was said to have been developed at Jouy, or at least to have been in use there after the idea had been brought from near Neuchâtel, by Oberkamphe's brother, Frederick. But in fact there are no surviving prints from the factory earlier than 1783. This press made it easier to produce lengths of fabric, but its working was such that continuous repeats could not be attempted easily. The particular difficulty in continuous-roll printing was caused by having to get the plate back through the rollers to its original position without winding the cloth back at the same time. This difficulty gave rise to the designs so printed at Jouy that are described as 'island' patterns because isolated scenes of pastoral, classical or topical subjects were skilfully arranged, often seeming to link but never, in fact, doing so. The repeat and registration problem was also one of the reasons for the use of only one colour.

A South East VIEW of the Cast Iron BRIDGE over the RIVER WEAR at SUNDERLAND in the County of DURHAM.

Not only do these illustrative copper-plate prints of the late eighteenth century, from England as well as France, show superbly how a designer can use the limitations and restrictions as well as the advantages and good qualities inherent in a technique to lead him into new ideas, but they are also examples of a designer using purely literal drawings to create highly decorative fabrics. The form and repeats are simply an outcome of the subject-matter and extend them satisfyingly and naturally.

It is in the history of Oberkamphe's factory that we first hear of designers by name, and the one who has left an unforgettable range of fabrics is Jean-Baptiste Huet, a talented painter and designer of the late eighteenth century. Huet's first design for the factory was rather appropriately *Travaux de la Manufacture*, showing all the various stages in the production of a piece of printed cloth.

To print fabric by this method, the first thing to do is to engrave the copper plate with the pattern, using a series of

This copper-plate-printed handkerchief depicting the 'South-East View of the Cast Iron Bridge over the River Wear at Sunderland in the County of Durham', 1796 (24 in. × 21½ in.), demonstrates the great wealth of textural and tonal interest which can be printed from an engraved plate.

gravers or burins. (This process is described in greater detail in Chapter 4, see p. 79.) After having its surface rubbed down and polished it is then ready for use. The engraved plate is placed on the heavy metal carrier which moves backwards and forwards so that the plate (with dye in its engraved surface only) passes in contact with and underneath an iron cylinder with a woollen covering. The cloth passes between the plate and the cylinder, and the cylinder revolves and presses the pattern out of the engraved portions of the plate and into the fabric. The plate then moves forward and is recharged with dye automatically, having the surface excess scraped off by a steel blade ('doctor'). Then the plate is raised to make its second contact with the cylinder. Because the pressure cylinder remains stationary (in between being rotated against the printing plate), the second impression can be started where the first leaves off, but, even so, exact and precise joinings are not possible. Note that in this process the cloth is *above* the printing device.

The finest and most beautiful copper-plate prints in England date from the mid-eighteenth century, but by about 1790 the quality seems to deteriorate. It is almost unbelievable that such precision and sharpness of detail could have been achieved with such comparatively primitive presses. Ironically enough, later in the nineteenth century, after Robert Kirkwood of Edinburgh had developed a much more sophisticated press, the quality of design fell even lower.

About 1785 many handkerchief and furnishing designs were printed in England for the American market, portraying American Independence and other aspects of American history. Copper-plate printing of handkerchiefs and scarves continued in Switzerland until as late as 1934 and the last commemorative print to celebrate Derby Day was printed in England in Kent, in 1946.

4 Engraved roller printing

Printing from an engraved plate is, as we have seen with copper-plate printing, an intaglio process, i.e. printing from lines cut into the metal. Briefly, it involves inking the plate, using some device for removing the surplus colour from the raised surface, and then applying pressure to transfer the pattern from the incised surface to the cloth. With the development of the engraved roller printing machine the rotary process is used; the copper plate becomes in effect turned round on to itself to become a cylinder and blades clear the top surface which has been supplied with colour from a trough. The cloth then receives an impression of the pattern by passing between the cylinder and a pressure roller.

Although the invention of the engraved roller printing machine is usually attributed to a Scotsman, Thomas Bell, who patented it in 1783, several other people in the previous thirty or forty years had patented versions which led up to the Bell machine. However, these prior patents did not include copper rollers or 'doctor' blades (used to scrape away surplus colour), and its seems fairly certain that his ideas brought together the only really workable solutions. In 1785 he sold his machine to Livsay, Hargreaves, Hall and Company in Lancashire.

It is often believed that the Industrial Revolution killed all skills and turned everyone into mindless machine watchers, but as Professor Ashton states in his analysis of the period: 'this is not only untrue, but the exact reverse of the truth.'* In all industries, the cotton industry included, highly trained machinists and maintenance men were needed and the engraved roller machine has always required a combination of skill and long experience for its successful operation. This must be remembered when reading the following description of a single-colour machine and the later one of the multicolour version, which apply equally to the first half of the nineteenth century and to the present time. There have been very few changes over the 150 years since the method began to be more widely used, and indeed none in principle. The power sources have changed, of course, water power giving way to steam, and that in its turn to electricity. And the new machines are made more streamlined in appearance, but many printworks are still using machines which have been in constant use since the nineteenth or early twentieth century.

*T. S. Ashton, *The Industrial Revolution 1760–1830*

A very early English engraved roller print, dated about 1815.

The single-colour roller machine

A single-colour engraved roller printing machine consists of the following parts. First there is a hollow cylinder on which the pattern is engraved (see pp. 76–97). Originally of solid copper, the cylinders are now all of the 'shell' type, having a thick deposit of copper on a steel core. After engraving, the cylinder is given a plating of chrome for extra strength. This plating increases the printing capacity of the roller by several hundred thousand yards, and has been a practice in the textile industry in Britain for the last twenty to twenty-five years. The cylinder is carried on a steel shaft, or 'mandrel', usually about a yard longer than the printing roller, with slots at the ends, into which the 'tabs' on the

Early nineteenth-century French roller-printed cotton from Marseilles.

69

inside of the roller fit when the two are forced together in a hydraulic forcing machine.

The cylinder rotates against a central cast-iron pressure bowl which is in fact the printing table. Around it is wound a specially woven and resilient fabric known as 'lapping', for elasticity. This has a linen warp and worsted weft and is an important feature in the production of fine and exact printing. In order to create the right kind of printing surface (or print table), about eight or ten thicknesses of lapping are wound around the pressure bowl; great care has to be taken to stretch it tightly enough and to ensure that it is free from creases. The ends have to be grafted together without ridging, and regular inspection is necessary to see that no detrimental change takes place in its surface which could cause differences in the strength of printing. The longer it is used, the less elastic it becomes, and gradually it has to be reserved for prints of greater fineness rather than more deeply engraved ones.

An endless woollen blanket also provides the extra resilience of surface needed for all forms of fabric printing. Originally these blankets were always of pure woollen material, but now they are often of the mackintosh variety. The 30 or 40 yards has to be made into an endless piece. To achieve this the ends are cut square and flat-stitched together with strong, fine thread – so perfectly that any fabric, however delicate, can pass over it and show little, if any, trace of unevenness on being printed. In recent years Mather and Platt, of Manchester, have used one of two blanket systems. One way is to have a long neoprene (synthetic rubber) proofed wash blanket, used with a back-grey (p. 37) over it, and sometimes also with a short woollen blanket which is situated between the central pressure bowl and the long blanket – for even more elasticity. The other system uses an extremely thick 'Darex' blanket (made in Mulhouse in France), which requires neither a back-grey nor a short blanket to give the necessary resilience. But usually there is a back-grey on top of the blanket; this is made of plain cotton and serves to stop any surplus dye from soiling the blanket. On top of this again is stretched the cloth which is to be printed.

Below the engraved cylinder is a furnishing brush – a cylindrical brush with bristles nowadays of nylon or fibre – or alternatively a furnishing roller, usually covered with matt rubber. This rotates in a 'colour-box'. Formerly these were made of wood, but they are now of copper or stainless steel (if necessary, sophisticated new ones can be made with ice-cavities for dyestuffs whose chemical composition is such that a low temperature must be maintained).

A traversing steel blade, or 'doctor' (originally often of gunmetal or German silver), screwed into contact with the copper cylinder, serves to scrape off the surplus colour from the raised, non-printing surface before printing. This cleaning doctor has to be kept extremely sharp, and it

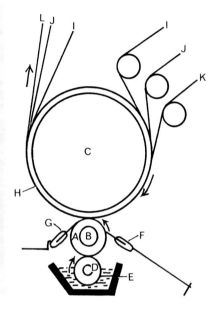

Diagrammatic section of a single-colour machine: A engraved copper roller; B mandrel; C pressure bowl; D colour-furnishing brush or roller; E colour trough; F doctor; G lint doctor; H lapping; I endless blanket; J back-grey; K cloth to be printed; L printed cloth.

traverses so as to prevent wear on the edge of the blade. If it stayed in one place, a particular design would affect the edge at certain points and stop the blade from functioning smoothly.

Finally, the 'lint doctor' is positioned so as to clear the copper cylinder of any fluff or streaks after printing. This is not always used but it is often necessary. It need not be so sharp or so finely set as the doctor, and it does not work with a traversing movement. Also, because the engraved cylinder moves towards this lint doctor, it can cause damage to the engraving if set at too sharp an angle.

And now for the machine in action. The engraved pattern roller rotates in an anti-clockwise direction and receives an excess of colour from the furnishing brush or roller, which having picked up colour from the trough, turns against the engraved roller clockwise. The surplus colour on the surface of the roller is then scraped off by the doctor blade, leaving it only in the engraved portions. This pattern is then transferred to the cloth by pressure as it moves along continuously through the machine with the back-grey and the blanket, between the engraved roller and the central pressure bowl. Continuing its anti-clockwise movement, the roller passes

(*Left*) The doctor blade, seen away from the machine.

(*Above*) A colour-furnishing roller of matt rubber, and a furnishing brush, also seen on a rack away from the printing machine.

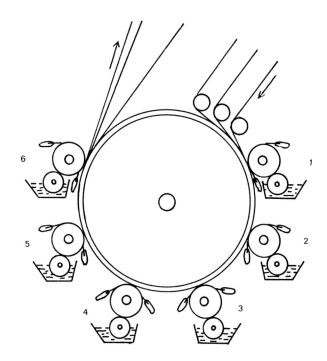

Diagrammatic section of a
multi-colour machine – in this
instance, one printing in six colours.
The 'nips' are numbered from the
back of the machine, the darkest
colours being positioned last. If a
'crush' roller is used, it is placed in
the last nip of all.

under the lint doctor and has any fluff cleared from its surface. The cycle is repeated indefinitely. When printed, the
cloth is then carried along into the drier.

The multicolour machine

Machines printing numbers of colours are a series of single-
colour units placed around one large pressure bowl, and
although more elaborate in detail, they do not vary in
principle. Thus a ten-colour machine has ten pattern rollers,
each equipped with its own furnishing brush or roller,
colour trough and doctor blades. All are driven by a single
crown-wheel on the side of the machine. Each roller works
in combined spring-and-lever adjustable bearings so that
while the machine is running at a slow speed the fit of the
various colours can be arrived at easily by slightly moving
the rollers up or down and also sideways. Because this
method allows only limited up-and-down movement,
later machines used a system of box-wheels, but this has now
been replaced by a helical pitching device (see p. 98). In
setting up a multicolour machine the printer places the
engraved rollers in tone sequence, with the lightest colour
in the first position (or the first 'nip' as it is called); this is
situated at the back of the machine. The reason for this
sequence is that because the surface of each subsequent
roller presses against the already printed cloth, smearing can
result, even though, as previously mentioned, the lint

doctor scrapes the roller clean after printing. However, if black or other dark colours were printed before very pale ones these would tend to become dirtied.

One of the disadvantages of engraved roller work is its lack of colour brilliance, caused by the crushing of the cloth during printing. Even the newest machines exert about 400 lb. pressure to get the printpaste (colour) out of the engraving, while in the older ones it was as much as 2,000 or 3,000 lb. So it is vitally important that the printer does everything possible to avoid further dulling of colour. Often a plain (unpatterned) 'crush' roller is placed in the last nip – this is needed occasionally to press in fairly large areas of colour and also to clear away the 'scumming' or 'bubbling' which can occur in an expanse of colour printed from an engraved roller. (Bubbling is caused by the continual churning up of colour by the doctor blade.) The most suitable designs for this process are those relying on a wealth of

Close-up of the machine while being set up. Note the plain roller in the top (last) 'nip': this is the 'crush' roller. The doctors and colour-boxes are not yet in position.

An old plate showing an early
Mather and Platt six-colour
engraved roller machine with a
double-cylinder diagonal engine.

(*Below*) An amusing nineteenth-
century American 'political' print,
showing the top hat and spectacles
of Horace Greeley, the unsuccessful
opponent of General Ulysses S.
Grant in his second presidential
campaign in 1872. Greeley was the
politician who gave the famous
advice, 'Go west, young man'.

finely drawn line detail, with a number of colours used in
small areas, and which do not contain large printed grounds,
or 'blotches'. In the early years of the nineteenth century
only machines which printed up to four or six colours were
designed, but as the century went on giant ones were built
that were capable of printing twenty or more colours.
Sometimes, though, in the early machines for more than
four colours, the colour-box was dispensed with and a
doctor was placed in a covered frame and applied to the
pattern roller instead. The doctor formed the bottom of the
colour receptacle and was strongly pressed against the roller;
the curved frame, stopped off at the sides with a piece of
copper curved to fit both roller and frame, and padded with
a piece of folded cotton cloth, formed the colour-box. This
type of box took up very little room and consumed little
colour.

Other cylinder printing machines

There are three important modifications to the ordinary
cylinder printing machine, all of which go back to mid-
Victorian times and are used today in the same form. The
'Duplex' which prints both sides of the cloth with the same
pattern; the 'Sari', or 'jumper', machine which prints two
different patterns intermittently; and the wax-printing
machines.

The *Duplex machine* was first in operation in England in
1875. You can print the fabric on both sides in one passage
through the machine, so that when in correct operation the
pattern on the back registers with the one on the front. Two
pressure bowls are used, placed diagonally to each other so
that there is the shortest possible distance between the last
printing unit on the first bowl and the first unit on the
second bowl. This reduces the tendency of the fabric to

stretch or to wander sideways. However, until the invention of the latest 'Aljaba' rotary screenprinting machine, Duplex (double-sided) prints were executed only on low-quality cloth and were highly textural and completely lacking in any refinement of registration. With the latest Aljaba rotary screenprinting machines, designs are cleaner and sharper and nearer the type of printing possible by other methods (see p. 133).

For printing *saris*, and items consisting of a piece of fabric varying in length from 2 to 12 yards, the *Sari, or 'jumper', machine* is used. Cross borders are usually required as well as a body or filling pattern, so an intermittent printing machine is necessary. This machine is designed so that some of the engraved rollers, known as 'heading' rollers, print cross borders at any distance from 2 to 12 yards apart. On completion of the cross borders the rollers are withdrawn from contact with the fabric. Similarly, the rollers which print the body pattern are withdrawn from contact at the cross borders. All the body and heading rollers, therefore, work

Another American 'political' print, a superb example of the fine detail and close fitting of colours it is possible to achieve in a good engraved roller print. This design depicts patriotic symbols – Liberty Bell 1776 and American Shield 1876 – and was printed in America in 1876.

The completed cylinder after being chromium-plated, showing the 'tab' which fits into the slot in the end of the mandrel.

intermittently according to the pattern to be printed. The rollers which print the side or running borders print continuously in the normal way.

To print batik-style designs there are *wax-printing machines* which use resin instead of wax, because of its cheapness and availability. These machines are of the Duplex type, enabling a resin pattern to be applied to each side. The mandrels, or steel shafts, for the engraved printing rollers are steam- or electrically heated and the special combined doctor and resin boxes are provided with a steam cavity.

ENGRAVING THE CYLINDERS

The engraved roller printing machine did not supersede block printing as quickly as one might have expected. By about 1840 there were only about 516 in the whole of the British Isles, whereas there were 7,873 block tables in England, 5,751 in Scotland and 584 in Ireland. The reason for the slow development (at first only the outline of the designs were engraved and the simpler colour areas filled in by block), was that the engraving of a copper cylinder by hand was an extremely slow process taking sometimes as long as several months. It was not until a mechanical means of engraving was perfected that a much faster change-over to the newer machines began – the first being 'mill', or machine, engraving in the 1820s, followed by the pentagraph in 1834. These cheaper and quicker methods paved the way for a gradual reduction of block printing.

The copper cylinder being given a final burnishing with a 'water of Ayr' stone. This makes the surface highly polished and ready for the fine engraving.

In an engraved roller printing machine, a hollow steel cylinder forms the core of the printing roller that I have already described in action. A collar of steel, into which a raised, straight 'tab' about $\frac{3}{4}$ in. wide and about 6–8 in. long has been cut, is then shrunk into the neck of one end of the steel cylinder; the purpose of this is to provide a key for locking in the mandrel, on which the roller rotates in the printing machine. The steel cylinder now has a coating of copper electrolytically deposited on its surface. (When copper cylinders were first made they were, of course, of solid copper and only later, when it became possible to coat satisfactorily with copper, were the 'shell' types used.)

Still supported on the mandrel, the rough copper-coated cylinder is placed in contact with an endless carborundum belt and a continuous jet of water. This smooths out most of the roughened surface. Then a final burnishing with a Water of Ayr stone makes the surface highly polished and equal to receiving fine engraving.

As previously mentioned, engraved roller printing is an intaglio process, the pattern being printed from colour held in the grooved surface of the copper and given up to the cloth by pressure. Originally, the engraved rollers were produced by engraving the copper, but the term 'engraved' has been retained for all intaglio printing surfaces, whether produced by engraving or etching. Nomenclature is conservative in the textile industry, where the Calico Printers retained their title even when printing on terylene, where a steam process of oxidization of dyes is called a 'rapid ager',

77

Using a punch to put in some extra detail on an already engraved cylinder.

and where even the process of producing a patterned silk screen is referred to as 'cutting' or 'engraving' a screen. Similarly, any coating applied to a cylinder to protect the surface during processing, is known as a 'varnish'. It may be light-sensitive, acid-resistant, or both, or it may be simply a 'ruling varnish', the function of which will be discussed later (see p. 86).

There are four main classes of engraving: hand engraving, which is hardly ever used now for a complete roller, but only in the correction of those produced by other methods or as a first process in the next two; mill or machine engraving; pentagraph engraving; and, finally, process or photographic engraving – a twentieth-century development after late nineteenth-century experiments.

It is important to remember that both mill and pentagraph engraving are carried on today in exactly the same way as when developed in the nineteenth century. In fact, as with roller printing, many of the old machines are still in constant use. Even though hand engraving is very little used today, it is necessary to be informed about it in order to understand the mechanical methods. For although the four

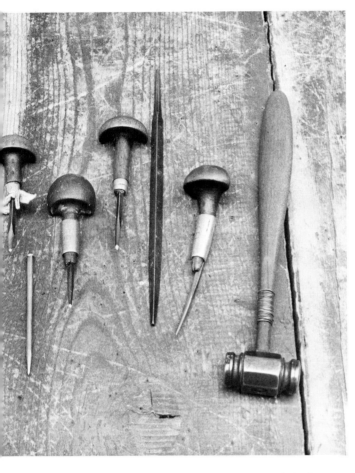

A set of gravers (or burins), punches and hammers used in hand engraving. The wire is used to fill in any small pits in the surface of the copper; it is hammered into the metal, and this is sufficient to key it in as the hammering causes the metal to spread.

classes are very different, the finished rollers, while showing subtle variations, are all basically the same and all do the job that hand engraving would have done previously.

Hand engraving

In this method the lines are cut into the surface of the copper by means of a 'graver' or 'burin'. (It is tradition in the textile industry that engravers still make many, if not all, of their own tools.) The graver consists of a cutting edge made from fine-quality steel bar, which is square or rhomboidal in section and slightly curved to enable the engraver to cut into the convex surface of the roller more easily. The handle of hardwood is round and shaped rather like a darning mushroom. These handles display individual characteristics because each man makes the shapes which suit his hand the best. You hold the handle of the graver in the palm of your hand and exert pressure from the palm and heel of the hand to drive it forward. The engraver also makes 'picking out' tools (used in repair work), punches of all sizes, and 'burnishers' from old files.

One of the delightful and characteristic features of an entirely hand-engraved copper roller was subtle shading produced by stippling the roller with small hammers or punches. Although this gave a well-controlled gradation of tone from the one roller the results were rather speckly, and so it was usual to print a flat, pale tone all over the stippling with a second roller. Sometimes a colourless paste only was used for this second printing and, falling on the wet stipple, it gave a subtle and smooth shaded effect. Until the 1950s when photographic engraving of rollers started to be more widely used in England, this hand method was the only means of producing gradation on cloth and was in fact one of the important qualities of roller printing. (Incidentally, it is worth noting that this is the only time in good-quality engraved roller printing when wet colour is allowed to fall on wet colour.)

The roller engraver, unlike the artist engraver, has to have a means of printing completely flat areas of solid colour, for flat shapes have always been an important characteristic of textile designs and are not easily created by engraving. They were only exploited fully in roller printing after mechanical engraving techniques had been developed. Flat areas of solid colour are arrived at by means of a series of parallel lines cut, at an angle of between $22\frac{1}{2}°$ and $30°$ from the horizontal, within the outline of the shape required. This angle is necessary to ensure that the doctor blade does not stick in the engraved lines (this point will be discussed more fully later, see p. 90). The number of these lines to the inch is known as the 'scale'. By varying the scale and depth of engraving you can vary the amount of colour put on to the cloth. In theory you would expect to be able to get all the tones of any colour from the very lightest to the most intense on one roller, but in practice it is only possible to rely on three or four, for factors such as consistency of printpaste and quality of cloth make a greater range difficult to achieve.

To return to the subject of wet colour, because the rollers representing each colour print in rapid succession, it is most important that any two adjacent colours in a design should be engraved with a very small gap between them; this will close up on printing, as a result of the slight spreading of colour which always occurs on cloth, particularly under pressure. This gap is known as the 'allowance' and because of the differing behaviour of various cloths in conjunction with printpastes (colour) of greater or less viscosity, its calculation is difficult and requires much experience. Too little space between colours causes 'bleeding' but too much leaves an unpleasant white line between shapes which will spoil a close-fitting pattern. The calculation is especially difficult when a fine black line is to be drawn around or through shapes of colour. To ensure a good, clean and correct print, a tiny line of unprinted cloth is left running through the colours in which the black line can be inserted

Close-ups of two engraved rollers
from a set, clearly showing how
areas of solid colour are represented
in parallel scale lines at $22\frac{1}{2}°$ to $30°$
from the horizontal.

without danger of 'flushing', or bleeding. (The allowance in
a screen print is almost always a small overlap – and will be
discussed on p. 119.)

Mill or machine engraving

The first development in engraving the cylinder, other than
entirely by hand, was mill engraving. In simple terms, a soft
steel cylinder, or 'die', is engraved and then case-hardened and
tempered. When this hardened steel is rotated against a soft
steel cylinder, or 'mill', a negative impression is obtained;
this in its turn is hardened before being used against the
relatively soft surface of the final copper roller. So, instead of
finely cutting the pattern directly into the copper roller it is
stamped into the surface by means of this previously prepared
mill with the design raised on it in relief.

Two pages of tiny mill-engraved cottons: (*above*) an original sample page showing black-and-white and black-and-purple patterns; (*opposite*) two examples of finely stippled flowers; a moiré background; a line-drawn fern pattern; and a mock ribbon design intricately engraved in black to give a bas-relief effect.

This type of engraving was, and still is, used for very tiny designs which, consequently, can have hundreds of repeats on the roller. And the invention of the process brought into fashion a host of minute florals, stripes and geometric and optical effects so beloved of the Victorian ladies of the 1840–80 period. These designs, preserved in pattern books and also perhaps more generally seen in the intricately assembled patchwork quilts of the period, have a fineness of drawing and wealth of varied detail which is staggering. It seems as if almost every conceivable dress fabric design must be represented in miniature in one or other of the manufacturers' pattern books. The inventor of the process, or perhaps more correctly, the developer, was John Potts who, until 1822,

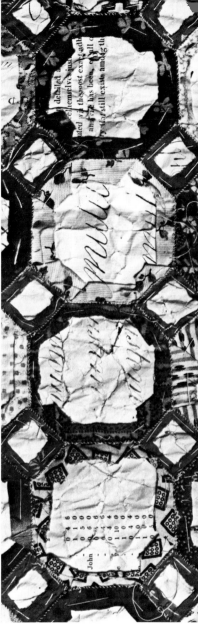

The back of an unfinished patchwork bedspread, showing how the Victorians used up old letters, accounts, etc. as a means of keeping the shapes 'true'. Often these were left in even when the coverlet was finished.

was working as a painter of pottery. He had a great reputation as a designer and was very familiar with the transfer system of putting fine lines and stipplework on pottery. In 1808 a method of machine engraving using a *flat die* had been introduced and tried out for fabric work. It had been originally developed by Thomas Perkins in America for the multiple printing of bank-notes. When John Potts moved to Derbyshire from the Potteries, bringing his design ideas with him, it was found impossible to engrave them using a flat die, because they were full of trails and sprays which interlocked, so requiring a continuous engraving technique. Thus, in 1824, he set up in business at New Mills, Derbyshire, where he developed a method for engraving the roller from

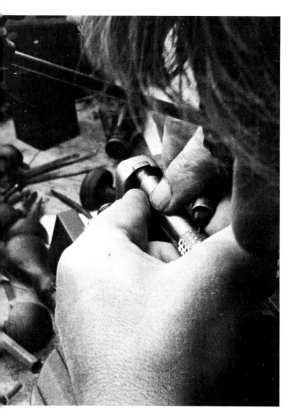

The first two stages in mill engraving: (*above*) the 'die' is engraved with the pattern exactly as if it was the printing cylinder; (*right*) after having had its outer surfaces punched all round to give a good holding surface, the die is hardened and then placed in the 'clamming' machine against a softened steel cylinder known as a 'mill'. So the pattern is transferred as raised images on the surface of the mill.

a cylindrical die and mill. A few years later the firm became Salisbury and Campbell. He was given a great deal of support by the Broadoak Printworks and the firm carried on successfully for nearly 150 years.

To prepare for mill engraving, the engraver traces the pattern to be engraved on to the soft steel cylinder (or *die*). The die will normally be as small as possible in circumference, sometimes no more than one repeat, but in any case the size of its circumference will be a factor of the circumference of the finished copper roller. One of several different methods for tracing can be used, partly determined by whether the design is a completely new one or not. When a new pattern is to be engraved, the engraver first draws the outlines of it on to a special 'oil paper', produced by soaking a proprietary wax paper in linseed oil. (Another type of tracing paper beginning to be used more is again of the wax variety, but it is given an extra coating of beeswax before it is drawn on.) The lampblack he traces with is easily transferred by burnishing from the paper to the surface of the die, which he has previously coated with a varnish made by boiling up resin with turpentine. Particular care must be taken to see that the tracing paper is tightly wound round the die, and in true alignment.

However, mill engraving is nearly always used for traditional patterns, such as stripes, spots and checks, and in such

The 'mill' seen in the engraving
machine transferring its pattern to
the copper cylinder.

cases an old die is used (instead of a drawing) as a means of
tracing off. The engraver takes an old die, engraved with the
correct pattern or portion of pattern needed to create the
new design, and into the engraved lines of this he rubs
lampblack. Then he rotates this die against the new varnished
one, thus under pressure transferring the outlines of the
design to it. Several different old patterns can be used to
help to create a new one, and by adding and subtracting
various elements endless permutations can be built up.

The die is then engraved with the pattern by hand exactly
as it would be if it were the printing cylinder itself. At this
stage the outer borders of the die, beyond the pattern area,
are roughly punch-stippled all round to provide a key so
that when it is put in the 'clamming' machine (the machine
used to apply the necessary pressure), it will remain in true
register and firm contact with the mill.

Next the die is case-hardened and tempered to make it
tougher than the cylinder against which it is to be pressed.
It is then placed in the clamming machine against this soft
steel cylinder, known as the *mill*. The mill is either the same
size as the die or larger, but still dimensionally a factor of the
final copper roller (it must be a fraction extra in circumference than the die to allow for the depth of the etching
which follows). A specially made black paste, which is
acid-resisting, is applied between the die and the mill in the

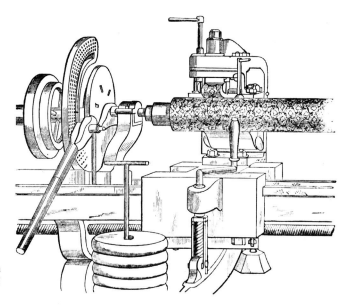

Machine engraving in the nineteenth century (*Practical Handbook of Dyeing and Calico-printing*).

machine; on rotation, this paste is then left in the engraved lines and the roughened borders of the die grip into the soft metal of the mill. With gradually increasing pressures, the pattern lines begin to be transferred on to the mill as raised images on which are coatings of black paste. This frictional contact in the machine is interspersed with several passages through baths of acetic acid and the acid–resistant paste protects the raised pattern lines, which are forming on the mill, during rotation in the acid. If excessive pressure only were used to raise the pattern on the mill to the necessary depth, the metal would suffer irreparable damage. Fatigue occurs fairly quickly as a result of pressure and so this combined process is adopted; while the pattern is slightly raised by pressure, the background is then etched away a little in the acetic acid. When the correct depth is reached, the mill has the raised borders turned so that they are smooth and well below the patterned surface.

The *copper cylinder* is coated with a special ruling varnish. It is then steamed and cured and fixed in the engraving machine where pitch marks are put on at the correct repeat distances by rotating a 'ruling' mill against the copper. Then the (raised) mill is fixed in the machine, in the first repeat position. This mill and the copper cylinder are now in frictional contact with each other and as the machine rotates the pattern is transferred to the copper roller by means of gradually increasing pressures. This time, pressure does not damage the roller because copper is a fairly soft metal. The engraved copper roller is now ready for printing.

The 'stipple' style of engraving, using tonal effects produced by a series of hammered punches (see p. 79), was much used in the period from 1824 to 1836, when Potts died, and mill engravings produced from dies so hammered were very popular. But by 1850 this style was little seen and, because it was (and still is) common practice to turn off a pattern in order to re-use the expensive copper rollers, all Potts's beautiful engraving has been lost.

Pentagraph engraving

This method of engraving uses the pantograph principle, but by tradition in the textile trade the process is known as 'pentagraph engraving' because originally the design was increased in size by five times. According to Knecht and Fothergill (see p. 185) the first successful pentagraph machine was Rigby's curved-table type of 1854. He used a principle discovered by an American named Whipple, which replaced the old pantograph idea of a parallelogram of pivoted rods connected by a movable slide and carrying a pencil or other drawing-point. Whipple's idea was based on the fact that if a large and a small wheel revolve together on the same shaft, any point on the circumference of the larger will cover a greater distance than one on the smaller. The idea of Rigby's machine and the less cumbersome flat-table one invented by Shields in 1857, was that the pentagrapher could, in one tracing over the enlarged pattern on the zinc plate, transfer to the surface of the copper roller as many repeats as he desired at one and the same time. The method not only had the advantage of speed but, because every colour of the design was first of all cut into one zinc plate and also enlarged, a high degree of accurate fitting could be attained.

A very early type of pentagraph.

The design to be engraved must be enlarged, usually three to five times. This is done now by a camera obscura which throws an enlarged image on to a whitened zinc plate. The pentagrapher draws a grid on both the paper design and the zinc plate and matches up the positions. He then traces all the design off and paints all the colours in so that there will be no mistakes on the rollers. Next on the zinc plate he engraves a line round all the separate colours by hand. Where two colours are intended to touch in the finished design, a double-toothed graver is used, the distance between the two points being the 'allowance'. As explained, the amount of space (or allowance) between colours must be finely calculated to ensure that on printing the colours touch without the wet areas bleeding into each other, but without being so far apart that a white line is left. It is essential that the engraving on the zinc plate should be very smoothly done as any roughness will subsequently stop the passage of the diamond points in the pentagraph machine.

Before being placed in the pentagraph machine the copper roller must be given a coating of acid-resisting 'trail' varnish. This is done by placing a metal roller and the roller to be engraved in a rotary machine, and spreading the 'varnish' over the metal one, which in turn coats the copper evenly. This so-called 'varnish' consists of a special blending of bitumen, gum mastic, and burgundy or black pitch,

The first stage in pentagraph engraving: after the enlarged design has been drawn on to the whitened surface of the zinc plate, it has all the colours engraved on it by hand (as shown here), a double-toothed graver being used to give the 'allowance' between colours.

(*Opposite, above*) The second stage: using the tracing-arm connected to the lines of diamond points in the pentagraph machine, the pentagrapher traces over the parts of the colour for each separate roller.

(*Opposite*) As the pentagrapher traces over the zinc plate, the diamond points only cut into the varnished surface sufficiently to lay bare the copper without actually cutting it.

mixed with turpentine. The zinc plate is now transferred to the pentagraph machine and the tracing arm connected to as many diamond points, in position around the copper cylinder, as are required for the particular design in work. As the pentagrapher traces over the parts of the colour for each separate roller, the diamond points only cut into the varnished surface sufficiently deeply to lay bare the copper without actually cutting it. When this job is complete the roller is taken from the machine and rotated in baths of nitric acid and then perchloride of iron.

There are several important points to note about the *etching process*. Firstly, the two acids have two distinct and separate functions. Nitric acid is used for widening and spreading while the perchloride of iron (ferric chloride) contributes depth to the finished work. The scale, as we have seen, is decided upon in relation to the tone required and how this will be best arrived at for the particular cloth and dye-stuffs to be used. But whatever this is, the finished roller must have space lines between each groove that are 0·002 in. in width. This amount of surface copper is necessary for support; any more would make an area of colour that was not smooth and even, but rather lined. Another feature of a colour roller is that the outlines of the large colour areas are etched to only half the depth decided on for the scale lines. This produces a sharp, defined edge. So, when the correct depth has been reached for the outline, the roller is taken out of the acid, washed, stopped out, then returned to the

machine to have scale lines added. The copper roller is then brought back to the acid troughs and the process repeated. Obviously, the judgment needed to assess the work at its different stages is something that is acquired only through a great deal of varied experience, even though depth gauges are used. Very few mistakes can be corrected.

When the etching is finished and the roller washed off in water, all the varnish must be cleaned off with a pure turpentine mixture or, more often, with naphtha. The copper must be burnished and made completely ready for use. If there are any small pits in the surface, these can be filled in with copper wire and rubbed down. The engraver simply snips off a tiny piece of wire and hammers it into the hole; this is sufficient to key it in because the hammering causes the metal to spread. All copper cylinders, these days, are chromium-plated, and immediately before this final plating extra burnishing and cleaning are necessary. The plating can easily make the cylinders last for an additional 100,000 yards of printing.

Before leaving discussion of the pentagraph machine there are three useful adaptations or ways it can be used that should be mentioned: the 'slash-arm' attachment which is no longer used; machines adapted to the production of two Duplex rollers simultaneously; the combined use of the machine and a 'ruling' mill in the production of some 'blotch' grounds.

As we have already seen, because of the action of the doctor blade, it is not possible to print horizontal lines, and therefore stripes, directly. These must be engraved at an angle of about $22\frac{1}{2}°$ and printed on the cloth which has first been 'stentered' out of true at the same angle. After printing and finishing it is brought back to correct tension, width and grain by restentering. A stentering machine is used in which, by gripping the two selvedges of the cloth with a series of pins, tension can be regulated, the finished width controlled, and the warp and weft made to run square or at any angle one to another. The degree of angle, if this is necessary, is termed 'slash'. This process of controlled distortion, or 'slashing', was made much more manageable by the 'slash-arm' attachment to the pentagraph machine, allowing the zinc plates to be made on the square and the engraving 'slashed' at an angle between $22\frac{1}{2}°$ and $30°$ on to

After etching, the hand-engraver makes small corrections to the pattern.

Diagrams to illustrate 'slashing' – the controlled distortion necessary to print horizontal stripes by engraved roller: A cloth in normal state with the warp and weft vertical and horizontal; B cloth after it has been distorted in the 'stentering' machine – the weft now lying at an angle of about $22\frac{1}{2}°$ from the horizontal; C cloth printed with the 'slashed' design; D after being washed and finished, the printed cloth has now been restored to normal by being restentered, the pattern of horizontal and vertical stripes appearing in the intended form.

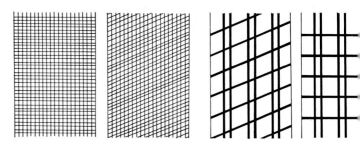

the roller. (For slashing in the photographic engraving process, see p. 92.)

The special pentagraph machines for engraving rollers for Duplex work have two sets of fittings to hold the rollers and two sets of diamond points which, working together, ensure that both copper cylinders are a perfect mirror-image match for each other.

Designs which have large blotches (printed grounds), and little pattern, can be more quickly produced by using a 'ruling' mill in conjunction with pentagraph work. The varnished roller is placed in the engraving machine and is ruled over its entire surface by rotation against a small mill which has the correct scale lines in relief upon it. Then the pentagrapher traces the outlines of any shapes not needed in the 'blotch' colour. These shapes are stopped out in black enamel and the cylinder is then etched to the necessary depth.

Occasionally, although rarely these days, a small piece of texture or a line of 'dragged brush' effect which it is impossible to copy in the pentagraph machine is put in by hand after the rest of the work is complete. This is known as a 'dry' line, because it is not etched. But it is only on rare occasions that this is used, as textural designs are so much more easily, and more satisfactorily, translated by photographic engraving.

Proving the cylinders in a 'strike-off' machine. They are tested for accurate fit and correctness of detail and while a cloth sample or 'strike-off' is sent to the customer, a portion is also retained as proof of the job.

'Dragged brush' effect.

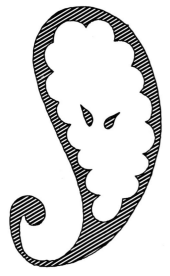

PHOTOGRAPHIC OR PROCESS ENGRAVING

As early as 1816, J. Nicéphore Niepce, who was a spare-time lithographer, decided to try drawing on metal plates coated with a layer of 'bitumen of Judea' dissolved in oil of lavender. He found that it did not work, but he then decided to expose the coated plate to the image in a camera obscura. After eight hours the bitumen became hard where the light was strongest and he was able to wash the rest off without disturbing it. He then etched the plate with acid and produced a crude picture which he called a 'heliograph' – although he had in fact pioneered photo-engraving. At the end of the nineteenth century, about 1893, experiments were carried out in the field of photographic engraving of copper cylinders for the production of textiles, and continued throughout the early years of the twentieth century. But it was not until the 1920s and 1930s that it was beginning to be commercially used. As far as England is concerned, in the late 1940s a few top firms were using it, but it was not till the late 1950s that it became widely employed.

The principle behind the method is that a full-size positive of each colour is made and wrapped completely round the roller which has previously been coated with a light-sensitive varnish. After exposing and developing, the roller is etched in the same way as before, the acid being able to reach only those portions of the design which are protected from the light source, and which, therefore, are not developed. This again is a very simplified explanation of a method which has many and varied aspects and problems.

Controlled distortion

Before embarking on a more detailed account of photographic work, it is necessary to deal more fully with two of the difficulties of engraved roller printing. First, because shrinkages in cloth width and length occur during the washing and finishing processes and these produce distortions of shape, it is often necessary to compensate by printing a slightly different shape in order to end up with a correct design, for example a circle needs to be printed as an oval; this adjustment is known as 'take-in' or 'pull-in'. Sometimes, also, the width of a design must be adjusted for other reasons, the normal pull-in being 1 inch in 36. Second, as mentioned previously (p. 90), weft-way (horizontal) stripes cannot be printed without 'slashing'; in such cases the copper cylinder is engraved with stripes set at an angle of $22\frac{1}{2}°$ from the horizontal and these stripes are then printed on to cloth which has been previously stentered out of true. Both the pull-in and slashing processes are made much easier by the use of photography, instead of the slash-arm attachment on a pentagraph machine. The Calico Printers Association, among others, have developed a machine for

(*Top*) Positive produced through line screen of the type used in photographic engraving of textile cylinders. (Note scale-lines at $22\frac{1}{2}°$.) (*Above*) Positive of the 'hard dot' type used for tonal work. (This does photographically the job the hand-engraver would do by 'stippling' with small punches and hammers.)

Two studio jobs: (*above*) touching-up a negative; (*left*) scribing a line on film – a method used to produce a very fine outline of even width.

this purpose. The negative is placed in one frame, and a film underneath in another, and each frame can move laterally or longitudinally. By independent movement of the film and negative under the light source (which is in the form of a very thin line), all necessary adjustments of width and angle can be made.

Photo-engraving the cylinder

The preparation of the positives (or sketches, as they are nearly always called in the textile trade) can be achieved in a variety of ways and will be dealt with more fully in relation to flat screen production in Chapter 6 (see p. 118). The only difference is that those positives which are used for engraved cylinder printing must have all the solid areas depicted in

Coating the cylinder with photographic emulsion: this would normally be done in a darkroom.

parallel scale lines. This is arrived at by photographing the hand-painted Kodatrace (or Permatrace or other plastic film) through a screen with lines again at an angle of $22\frac{1}{2}°$ from the horizontal.

A woman worker painting-out parts of the pattern on the cylinder prior to etching (*Practical Handbook of Dyeing and Calico-printing*).

Before exposure, the cylinder must have a coating of photographic emulsion, or 'varnish', put on in a darkroom. The varnish is fed through a pump on to a chamois leather tongue, which traverses very slowly, spreading it evenly as

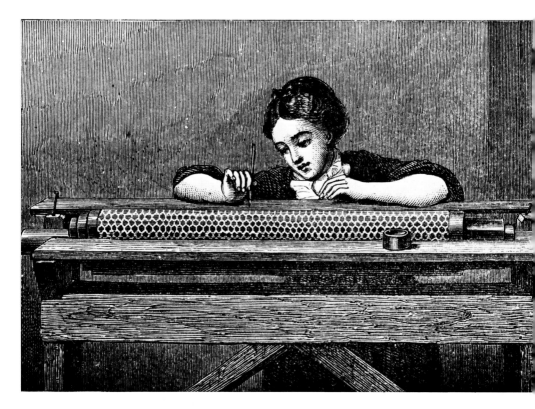

the cylinder rotates. There are other methods of coating, of course, notably the use of a machine which holds the cylinder vertically and covers it by means of a cylindrical doctor which is automatically fed with a controlled amount of the photographic emulsion. It must be remembered that for the cylinders which are to take very fine engraving, a fine coating of emulsion is given, but for coarser work more covering is required and a second coating may be applied. The cylinder is then dried and placed in a rotary exposing cabinet.

The operator wraps round the cylinder a positive of the same size as the cylinder and on top of this tensions an apron of clear plastic to prevent any light creeping through. He brings the light source closer (it is usually situated both at the top and the bottom) and rotates the cylinder for the correct exposure. (This time varies according to the character of the pattern on each particular roller.) After removal of the film, he transfers the cylinder to a trough of developer and then washes it off with a spray of water. Since the areas to be etched are now laid bare and the areas to remain are protected by varnish, one would expect to take the roller to be etched at this stage. Instead, it is necessary to give the surface of the copper extra protection by hand painting, and black enamel is brushed in over the parts that are not required to be etched away. The copper cylinder is then etched in the manner previously described for pentagraph work.

Between developing and etching, it is necessary to give the background areas the extra protection of a coat of black enamel; this is brushed on by hand.

Rotating the cylinder in the acid
bath.

Which engraving process?

At first glance it would seem reasonable to assume that the
widespread adoption of photographic methods in the engraving of copper rollers would immediately supersede
any other method. The nature of photography is such that
anything can be photographed, and certainly almost any
effect can be separated, by one means or other, a positive
made and a cylinder subsequently 'engraved'; and this can
have a wide variety of linear, textural and tonal qualities.
However, both mill and pentagraph work are still produced in quite large amounts, in England. Greater speed,
the lower cost of production or even the character of the
pattern to be printed are all factors which provide an
explanation for this.

Very tiny designs, as mentioned before, are ideal for mill
engraving although the pentagrapher can adequately cope
with repeats of up to $\frac{1}{2}-\frac{3}{4}$ in. Why, though, should they not
be produced much more quickly by photographic means?
The reason is that fine, small-scale all-over linear effects, in
particular, are very difficult to engrave evenly over the
necessarily large surface of a copper cylinder. However well
controlled the timing devices on a 'step-and-repeat' machine
may be, shading tends to occur at repeat junctions. Mill
engraving, being a rotary repeating method, in the hands of

Using a depth-gauge to check the etching.

skilled engravers and other operatives eliminates this difficulty. Also, certain small-scale geometric patterns which would seem to be a good scale for pentagraph work are sometimes better done by mill if a particularly sharp angular character is needed in the engraving; at present the shading aspect would again possibly rule out photography.

One positive advantage of photography, though from a purely design viewpoint, is the comparative ease with which tonally shaded effects can be produced. These design qualities were previously only possible by lengthy hand stippling with a series of small punches and hammers. Now, although there is a little use of mill-engraving, photographic engraving is the usual method, always bearing in mind that rotary screen printing has become the most important method of textile printing.

TWENTIETH-CENTURY DEVELOPMENTS

Several of the engraved roller machines in use in England today are very old indeed, dating back to the end of the Victorian era, while the new ones, although more stream-lined, are not really different in principle, as we have seen. But Mather and Platt, the Manchester engineering firm still producing engraved cylinder machines, in 1956 introduced two subtle improvements – a helical pitching device, and also hydraulic loading.

The helical pitching device

This device eliminates the 'box-wheels' which were previously used to adjust the roller when, although perfectly parallel, it is printing a little below or above its correct position. If this happened, it was not lifted or lowered bodily in its bearings, but by having its speed of revolution briefly decreased or increased the roller was brought into correct fit without having its pressure against the central bowl disturbed. The new helical device also works to cause a slight momentary acceleration or deceleration in the drive being transmitted to the mandrel. A single turn of a hand-wheel gives approximately 1 mm. pattern movement, and once correctly adjusted the assembly can be locked in position with no possibility of later movement out of true. The new system has the economic advantage, too, of accommodating rollers of widely varying diameters and of being safe in operation and less time-consuming than the older box-wheel device.

Hydraulic loading

This more sensitive method of loading allows the pressure applied on each side of each printing roller to be separately adjusted, measured and recorded so that operating conditions can be repeated accurately day after day. As a result of controlled loading, the expensive lapping on the central bowl retains its active life much longer and the time saved in bringing the engraved rollers evenly to the printing bowl is greatly reduced. (Although this ability to record and repeat pressures helps greatly, in practice it is not always as easy to repeat conditions mechanically as one would expect.)

The Saueressig machine

In the early 1970s a completely revolutionary engraved roller printer was designed by Saueressig of Ahaus in Germany, its main attraction being the ease of operation and servicing. There is a feeling among textile people that if this machine had come along about eight or ten years sooner it might well have altered the course of fabric printing development, in that it might have swung the interest away from rotary screens and slowed down their development. In any event, its advantages were sufficiently obvious to inject new blood into the older industry.

The conventional cylinder machines produce extremely fine and high-quality prints, but to do so they require expert handling by men with years of experience. The

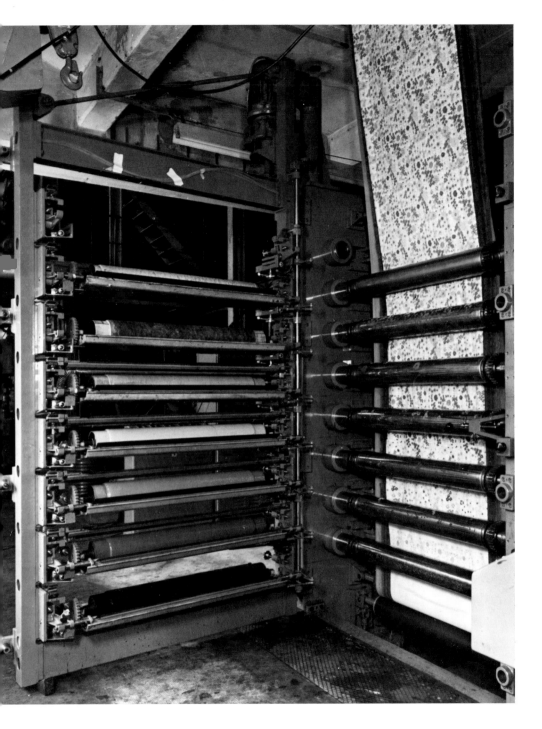

The revolutionary Saueressig engraved roller printing machine with the hinged 'colour gate' open. The photograph clearly shows how the colour units consisting of colour-furnishing rollers, doctor blades and colour-boxes are arranged in a rectangular metal frame which is here swung out from the rest of the machine and out of contact with the pattern rollers.

emphasis in recent years, rather sadly perhaps, has been on machinery so skilfully designed and so foolproof in operation as to need tending only by quickly trained and inexperienced operatives. The feeling about the cylinder machine, in America particularly, was that 'if it didn't become more scientific and need less art and less printer's skill, it would become obsolete and go the way of the Model T'.

The claim for the new Saueressig machine is that it does not rely on human judgment, but that the quality of production is scientifically controlled by instruments. But it is not the fact that there is a panel to control all the operations of the machine, and that one can record the fitting and pressure of rollers in order to duplicate conditions for repeat orders, that singles this machine out; similar controls are built into all the latest models of roller printing machines. It is something far more revolutionary in principle that makes it a very important contribution to the engraved roller printing industry.

Instead of having a central pressure bowl around which the printing units are arranged, the machine is of vertical design with multiple pneumatic pressure rollers, one for each printing cylinder. Each pressure roller is part of a single printing unit and these units are stacked one on top of the other to form a multicolour printing machine. No mandrels are needed to support the pattern rollers, but only side supports.

But the most revolutionary aspect of the new design, resulting directly from the vertical arrangement, is the movable, hinged 'colour gate'. All the colour units – consisting of colour-furnishing rollers, doctor blades and colour-boxes – are arranged in a rectangular metal frame which can be swung out from the rest of the machine and out of contact with the pattern cylinders; so, as well as being easier to service because they are all at the front of the machine, a great deal of extra time is saved because a second operator can, at the same time, clean the furnishing rollers and troughs. The colour-boxes are supplied by an air-pumping system which automatically controls the colour levels, as indeed also in screenprinting machines. It is claimed that the set-up time for a six-colour design is thirty minutes, although in practice it is nearer an hour. This is a considerable advance on the conventional machine which can take about three to four hours. More time is saved by the fact that four rollers at once can be lifted in a cradle, and on pushing a button they are engaged.

There are several other good points about the design, for instance the lack of mandrels, which is considered advantageous not only because of a saving in money (for they are costly items), but because when they are used great pressure is exerted on the ends, resulting in a slight distortion in the surface of the engraved cylinder. In the Saueressig, because of the precision straightness of the surface of the printing cylinder, the doctor blades can be prepared in an accurate

English plate-printed cotton, 1761.

Examples of Victorian mill-engraved
dress prints, showing the use of
different dye styles.

grinding machine, with only a little hand finishing. In the past the regrinding of the blade was a highly skilled hand-controlled job. Again, air pressure controls the contact of the doctor blade and the increased efficiency that results produces much more even blotch grounds, particularly when these are large in area.

The printing pressure is regulated by the setting of an air-pressure gauge and the rubber-covered back-up cylinders can be retracted individually, also by air pressure. This means that, unlike the older models, little pressure is needed to give a good print and so a lot of the dulled colour which is a consequence of greater pressure is avoided. Colour is cleaner and brighter and more on the surface and the results are more like screen work. The cut in colour consumption is about 20 or 30 per cent.

The print rollers can be put into exact repeat before printing, but adjustments can also be made while the machine is in work. The machine does give faster produc-tion speeds, not because it is necessary to 'blind along' but because the set-up time is reduced by at least half. It is never desirable, anyway, to run a machine too fast, as then it is impossible to observe the quality of the print.

One of the other drawbacks of the older style of engraved roller machine was that a lot of 'seconds' were produced during colour-changing and pitching, but in this new machine, because each roller can be quickly retracted by the push of a button, this is largely avoided. If it is necessary to stop the machine for any reason, the operator can release the back-up rollers and keep the printing cylinders rotating without using colour: this stops drying-in of the print-paste in the engraved portions of the pattern. Stopping results in only about 3 yards of 'seconds' instead of possibly something in the region of 30 yards. Another point about the quick retraction of the rollers is that if, say, one wants to take out the blotch roller, one can just press a button and do so immediately, again without much spoiling. This speed and ease of set-up means that it is possible to use it as a sampling or 'strike-off' machine, thus saving the expense of a separate one. It is really economic for short runs as well as long ones.

When we come to the section on rotary screen printing (p. 131), it will be seen that the advantages claimed for the Saueressig are almost identical to the points in favour of rotary screenprinting machines – short set-up times, easy operation by quickly trained workers, and economic operation for short as well as long runs. Combine these advantages with the fact that engraved copper cylinders are stronger and therefore possibly longer-lasting than the more fragile metal mesh of rotary screens, and it is not difficult to understand that it is much more competitive with screen work than was the conventional roller machine. The Saueressig will certainly bring about a rejuvenation in the engraved roller industry, particularly in the United States,

(*Opposite, above*) A patchwork quilt in blockprinted and engraved roller-printed fabrics.

(*Opposite, below*) Modern Dutch engraved roller prints in the 'African' style.

and also probably in areas where there is no tradition of the older work. Photographic engraving of cylinders can be used, if desired, for all classes of work, and this stage, too, can be given a high percentage of automation, dispensing still further with long training and experience.

The Saueressig machine is also extremely well adapted for the printing of knitted fabrics, many of which are impossible, or at best extremely difficult, by conventional means. Speeds of up to 40 yards per minute can be reached, as compared with about 70 yards for woven cloths. From its first showing at the Paris Textile Machinery Fair in the summer of 1971, twenty of these machines were sold in the first year, so it would seem that it is already beginning to satisfy a definite need in the textile industry.

5 Lithographic printing

Already we have seen two main printing techniques: relief and intaglio. There is, however, a third category, rarely applied to textiles but used extensively for paper printing, that is surface or lithographic printing. In this process there is no difference of depth between the printing and non-printing surfaces. In simple terms the principle is as follows. The design is prepared in greasy ink upon a porous surface, such as limestone or roughened metal. If then the damp surface is supplied with a film of varnish printing colour, the clean portions will repel it and the greasy ones be reinforced. Impressions may be obtained from this inked design just as in relief printing.

As far as paper printing is concerned, no difficulty is experienced with suitable inks when printing from hard surfaces, because even a very thin film of ink is sufficient to carry the amount of pigment required for the printing of a solid colour. But, because even fine fabrics need a fair amount of colour to penetrate the cloth, it would seem to be difficult to make the lithographic method work on textiles. In block printing, 'felting' is used to aid colour retention and the cavities in the surface of an engraved roller can be etched deeply enough to hold dye-paste in sufficient quantity for each type of cloth to be printed. Although lithographic printing by its nature precludes this method, difficulties are not so great as one would imagine, as the necessarily greater amount of colour may be applied to the design areas and penetrates the cloth well, whereas the same amount on paper would blur and spoil the image.

Lithography is a chemical process. The original limestone has now been generally replaced with zinc or aluminium plates, but unless the greasy areas of pattern are given a chemical treatment successive printings will deteriorate rapidly. The greasy ink in which the design is prepared is a mixture of wax, soap, a drying oil and black pigment, and is applied either directly to the printing surface or to a paper having a soluble coating – 'transfer paper' – and then transferred to the printing surface. Nitric acid then acts on the soap to release the fatty acids and also on the clean areas of the stone to make it more capable of moisture retention. When metals are used they are treated in other ways to produce similar results. Dyestuffs were not used with this method, but instead a pigment colour with a drying-oil medium, which was absorbed by the cloth with comparatively little stiffening.

Lithography from thin metal plates was used for handker-chief printing but the only rotary method there has ever been was Hayes's lithographic machine, in which cylinders of zinc or aluminium were roughened and the continuous design transferred on to them. It was also possible to have a machine which would print up to four colours. One impor-tant feature of the process was the cheap method of making the pattern rollers and the ease with which the pattern could be wiped off and the roller re-used. Only the original small plate with which to print the transfer paper needs to be retained. The machine consisted of a rubber-covered pressure bowl with which the design cylinder was in contact. Colour was furnished from the trough by a series of rollers and the printing cylinder was kept damp by two other rollers specially placed for the purpose. The Hayes machine was much simpler to operate than ordinary litho-graphic machines, and printed about 60–80 yards per minute.

An older form of lithographic printing for transfer work was known as 'decalcomanie', and was used for such things as embroidery transfers. The design was printed on paper and required the application of heat for transference. Lithography will be referred to again in Chapter 7 since it is one of the four methods used to print the transfer paper for transfer printing.

6 Screen printing

The start of the twentieth century saw the British textile industry in a flourishing state. For instance, in 1901 the production of printed and dyed textiles amounted to 1,326 million yards, of which 91 per cent was exported. The figure will mean more if one compares it with 1964 when only 272 million yards were produced, only 32 per cent being exports. In 1899 the Calico Printers' Association had been formed, and at the beginning of the century this consisted of about forty-seven printworks. But the period after the First World War brought about a depression here as in other manufacturing countries and in 1928 closure of some works had already begun. In the 1930s James Morton, a member of the outstanding Scottish textile family, wrote:

> Lancashire manufacturers instead of settling down to become rich land-owners, should have been ready with new developments in the artistic, chemical, and mechanical sides of the industry, against the situation that now faces them, when the rest of the world is suddenly alongside or ahead of them in their own game.

And it is certainly true that all the major developments in printing techniques during this century have emanated from European countries – Germany, Holland, Austria, France, Switzerland, Italy and even Portugal – although great developments in dyestuffs have been made in England.

The most significant contribution of the century to textile printing development has been hand screen printing and its various mechanical derivatives; but it is the hand process that has so changed the character of design in fashion and furnishing fabrics all over Europe.

The great importance of hand screen printing as an industry is that it affords the creative and imaginative designer the means of putting on cloth extremely varied ideas and effects. Because the pattern was (and often still is) painted by hand on to a plastic film, or 'Kodatrace', and the screen developed directly from this, it follows that there is virtually nothing that can be painted on paper that cannot be screenprinted on cloth. This broad generalization needs little qualification in practice, because there is really no conversion process, as in cutting a block or engraving a copper cylinder.

A very early screen print by Edinburgh Weavers, produced in 1935 and designed by Hans Tisdall.

The development of hand screen printing was encouraged in the 1920s and early 1930s by the need to find a method of printing new designs for the 'art silks' and other viscose and acetate rayons. For these new 'high fashion' cloths a process was required which would print, easily and less expensively, greater yardages than could be managed by the slow hand block method, and yet not so great as were needed for economic roller printing. That is why, in this instance, hand screening was an extremely suitable medium, both from the yardage point of view, and also because the new freer styles of pattern and the glowing colours so right for the mood of the period were easily attainable in this way.

During the 1930s, 1940s and early 1950s, English and European couture houses made great use of screenprinted silks and fine wools. In the 1930s the first Sundour screenprinted range of furnishing fabrics was produced. At this time, too, the British textile industry was injected with new blood from Europe in the form of refugees from Czechoslovakia, Austria, Germany, Hungary and elsewhere, who brought with them not only great technical skills, but more important still for designers, a creative new approach to colour and pattern. They, along with the more enlightened British producers, used skills in screen printing to further the design standards of British fabrics. Firms such as Edinburgh Weavers, Allan Walton Textiles, Heal's, Ascher, Wardles of Leek and Horrockses Fashions gradually began to make Britain known for the production of new, pace-making designs and quality fabrics, rather than of vast yardages of cheap cloth for home consumption or export to a passive Empire market.

Opposite:
A screenprinted fabric designed by Duncan Grant for Allan Walton Textiles, 1938. The design shows superbly the freeing influence of hand screen printing, and the interesting effects possible when fabric can thus be printed directly from the painted tracing, without an intermediate translating process.

For many years, from about 1930 until the late 1950s when photographic engraving of copper rollers was beginning to be more universally used in Britain, hand screen printing was the only method whereby experimentally drawn designs could be carried out on cloth. This fact, coupled with the ease with which colourings could be changed and the comparatively low cost of making screens, was largely responsible for a radical change in design styles.

Alastair Morton, one of the great pioneers of hand screen printing in this country, created for the Britain Can Make It Exhibition in 1946 a series of fabrics from a group of basic screens: horizontal and vertical stripes, straight or wavy stripes, stars, flower-heads, polka-dots, rings – each being on the same module. He showed the immense versatility from simple elements which was possible by screen printing but could not be achieved by any other process. In the same year, Morton joined Horrockses Fashions, a firm set up in England to pioneer new ideas in fashion cottons. This was to be a highly successful attempt to give cotton back its importance as a quality printed fabric. Edinburgh Weavers had been started in 1923, but it was not until the Paris Exhibition of 1937 that the new range really gained an important place in European design. After the Second World War (in 1955), the range had a great rejuvenation with a wonderful series of fabric designs commissioned from artists and designers from all over Europe.

Hand screen (or table printing as it is known in the US) is still used in Europe for the printing of silks, woollens and high fashion fabrics for couturiers and others, and for silk scarves and shawls e.g. Antonio Ratti and Mantero Como. The other very important field is in the production of small runs of 'decorator' fabrics and contract work for architects e.g. Manufacture del Impression sur Etoffes (M.I.E. Rîbeauvillé in Alsace and others) who produce cotton fabrics printed in 20/30 colours by this method. A type of printer being used more and more widely in Europe by the hand printers is the 'carriage printer'. This was first developed by Galli, a Spanish company, in the 1960s. At present, many types and sizes, such as the large Viero are in use for scarves, shawls and panel designs. They have sophisticated computer controls of squeegees, speed and pressure, as well as repeat size. They are used to produce 'handpoints' of ever-increasing fineness, combining all the best features of handscreen printing with the exactness and control of automation.

FROM STENCILS TO SCREEN PRINTING

Screen printing is basically a stencil process. But, whereas in a children's stencil outfit the waxed paper stencils have to have fairly large 'ties', making 'free' shapes impossible, in screen printing any kind of shape is printable, because the mesh of the basic screen, either silk, nylon or metal mesh,

provides ties so fine as to be invisible when colour is pressed through. But all modern screen printing can be traced back to the use of stencils – an art brought to a high level of excellence by the Japanese.

(Above, left) An automated 'carriage' printer.

(Above, right) A Japanese dyeing stencil, showing the intricacy of cutting and the fine linkings.

Japanese stencils

The introduction of the stencil plate into Japan as a means of patterning fabric probably occurred at the end of the eighth century. Even though the technique was such a primitive one the Japanese achieved, and still achieve, amazingly fine detail and intricacy of pattern with stencils. They also developed the idea of strengthening the fragile webs of paper (often so elaborately cut as to be nearly all holes) with ties of human hair or fine untwisted silk. These fine linkings either did not show or were so slight as not to matter. Some of the earliest fabrics were produced by clamping the fabric between two boards cut with the pattern and which fitted exactly into each other. With this seemingly primitive method very intricate patterns were produced. When one looks at the stencils it is impossible to see that they do, in fact, consist of two layers of paper, identically cut and between which the hair or silk threads have been sandwiched to provide a little extra strength and support. The colour is gently pressed through with a large soft brush, which must be of the right resilience to prevent damage to the stencil, or breakage of the ties, yet not so soft as to force the colour underneath the edges.

Many variations are possible from one stencil, but the basic ones are those obtained by brushing the colour (often indigo) through in the way described – and the reverse, by rubbing a resist paste of rice, usually with a spatula, into the parts not protected by the stencil, and subsequently dipping the cloth in a dye-bath. The resist is then cleared away by washing.

The exquisite effects produced can be made even more exciting by a variety of hand-painting techniques, often by the subtle shading of animal and plant motifs. Some of the more elaborate cloths were prepared with innumerable stencils: with directly applied dye combined with the use of resist and free-hand painting, and later enhanced with embroidery in gold and coloured threads. In the nineteenth century the stencil work was the sole method of 'printing' in Japan and many thousands of very beautiful designs on cotton, crêpe and silk were produced.

Sheets of strong paper made from mulberry fibre, which was then waterproofed, were used for the stencils. The craftsman would put about six sheets together, and on top of these he would place the paper design. The sheets were fastened together firmly with the pins and then he would cut them with a long, thin knife, pushing it away from him just as the engraver does when using a burin. Dots, if needed, were made with a punch.

When the design had been cut, the cutter took two of the sheets and dampened them thoroughly; one was then brushed with an adhesive and the fine threads or hairs (for extra strength) were laid across the complete stencil in several directions. On top was placed another stencil, its position being correctly determined by putting pins through the registration holes previously marked on all six sheets together. When new stencils were needed (and none lasted very long), one from the first group was placed on the new pile of paper and used as the master from which to cut a fresh set.

But while this technique, used to decorate fabric, reached unprecedented heights in Japan, it was from early times a means of repeating patterns on walls, furniture and floors in as many varied places as Ancient Rome, Norman England, medieval Europe, and more recently in America, as well as in tribal cultures like Fiji, where it was used to pattern bark cloths.

As far as America was concerned, walls and floors were decorated this way in the late eighteenth and nineteenth centuries by itinerant decorators. There was a fashion for velvet pictures, decorated with rich baskets of fruit and flowers, and chairs, tin trays and boxes patterned in bronze powder as well as colours. In America, too, a certain amount of textiles were stencilled (in pigment colours, not dyes), as the illustration overleaf of the bedspread shows.

In the late nineteenth and early twentieth centuries, particularly in France, metal stencils or *pochoirs* were made.

Zinc or copper plates were varnished and the pattern then traced on to them. The outline was engraved with a sharp tool and mastic was put round the edges to stop the acid from spoiling them while they were deeply etched. Then the unwanted part was pushed out, leaving a stencil which was washed in cold water to remove the mastic. An 'aerograph' spray was used to finely shade colour through the stencil on to the cloth.

A beautifully stencilled Japanese garment, patterned with birds, and irises and other water plants.

An unusual use of the stencil technique shown here in a nineteenth-century American bedspread. The use of stencilling in America last century was widespread and various, and the colours employed were oil-based pigments, not dyestuffs.

According to research carried out by a writer for the *CIBA Review*, the first stencil prints which make the change-over to silk gauze, or in other words to a continuous form of support, were made in 1850 at Lyons. Only very small quantities of each design were made. In 1870 screen prints began to appear in Switzerland and Germany, but none of them was any more than experimental.

It was in 1907 that a Manchester man took out a patent for a screenprinting process, and during the First World War Stars and Stripes banners were printed by this method. But not until about 1926, in Europe, did screen printing begin to take the form of an industry.

Although engraved roller printing was of course much cheaper by comparison, provided large quantities of a particular design were required, hand screen printing still had many advantages, particularly for a designer. The cost of setting up a design was considerably less, and also much speedier. It was a simple operation to change a set of colours and, for exclusive designs of more unusual quality, the advantages are obvious.

HAND SCREEN PRINTING

When screen printing was first developed it was done entirely by hand. A frame of wood was stretched tightly with fine silk or organdie, on to which the pattern was transferred. A fabric known as 'bolting silk' which had been created for flour-milling sieves was used for a number of years. The warp threads in this special silk were fixed in position between two twisted weft threads, so ensuring a completely stable base on which to engrave a pattern. (It should be remembered here that the term 'engraving' or 'cutting' is used to indicate the transferring of a pattern to the screen, even though engraving as a craft is not in any way involved; this term is a 'throwback' to the older copper cylinder printing.) This transference of the pattern was, and still can be, done in a great variety of ways – from the extremely simple one of painting out the background with varnish (as practised in some schools) to the most advanced of photomechanical techniques.

The tables were originally heavy wooden ones covered with a thick felt and a washable cotton backing cloth. (A

Small screen printing tables suitable for a college installation. Notice the guide-rails and stops on the sides for registration purposes.

resilient surface is absolutely essential for good fabric printing, whether screen, block or roller.) It was soon discovered that metal tables were needed because the wood quickly warped, and this tended to make for uneven impressions. The newer tables were also equipped with special adjustments to cope with uneven floors. About 60 yards is the maximum length of table needed for efficiency; for a variety of reasons longer lengths do not really have any added advantage.

On one side of the tables a system of guide rails, stops and brackets now enables the printer to obtain correct registration of each screen; these connect with brackets or screws in the screen frame which can be further adjusted when the screen is in position and in almost correct register.

Wooden screen frames soon gave way to more stable and durable ones made of metal. Originally the 'squeegee', or doctor used for pressing the colour through the screen mesh, was entirely of wood also, but then hard rubber blades were found to be more satisfactory and so these were inserted into the wood. The squeegee is an important piece of equipment. It must be constantly checked to make sure that the blade is perfectly true, any irregularity producing an uneven print. One, two or more strokes are used, depending on the depth of colour required.

Adapting the design

The following notes on preparing a design for screening apply equally to preparing one for any other repeat process, but this is a suitable place to insert the details of correcting repeats because hand screen printing is a method widely practised in schools and colleges.

As we have already seen, it is possible by screen printing to reproduce on cloth almost any effect, providing the time, the skill and the correct fabrics, and other equipment, are available. But, in practice, the fact that almost anything can be screenprinted can present design problems, in that one can reproduce a 'one-off' painting in repeat in such a way that it bears no relationship to a length of cloth but still remains a set of separate, unrelated motifs, not integrated in any way into a complete whole. Alastair Morton wrote in the *SIA Journal*:

> Every detail of [Henry] Moore's designs (as reproduced) has the appearance of a drawing on paper. The lines have the subtlety of a deft finger-stroke, not the wide sweep of an arm over a linen canvas six feet by nine. . . . The latest methods of photographic screen-making for printing textiles are so automatic, so facile, that they make possible, even encourage, the most shocking slickery.

Morton was commenting on the large printed linen panels by Ascher and criticizing them for being 'such faithful (enlarged) reproductions of artists' drawings'.

As far as skill is concerned, the job of the reproduction artist or colour separationist is probably the most important of all. Certainly, if this part of the job is not well done nothing else is likely to be successful. It takes about eighteen months to two years to train a man fully for the job and after that, if working in a firm producing varied work, he needs at least three to five years' experience before he is capable of making all decisions about the various methods to use for any particular design.

A one-colour design by Anne Mackinnon, a final-year student of the Manchester Polytechnic, showing repeat crosses drawn in and a cutting line indicating the repeat limits to be painted on the tracing.

(1) Draw a line through point x to the same point (y) on the next repeat; (2) draw a line from x at right angles to xy. This should pass through the same point (z) on the lower repeat. (If it does not, the inaccuracy in the design can be rectified later.) (3) Through y make a line parallel to xz, and through z one parallel to xy; (4) divide this repeat rectangle into quarters. (5) In the centre of a new piece of paper draw two crossing lines; (6) cut out the quartered repeat and stick the quarters down on the new paper in diagonally reversed positions i.e. centre corner *a* is now placed in what was corner *ci*. The outer limits of the repeat are assured of accuracy because they are now the cut edges from the centre area.

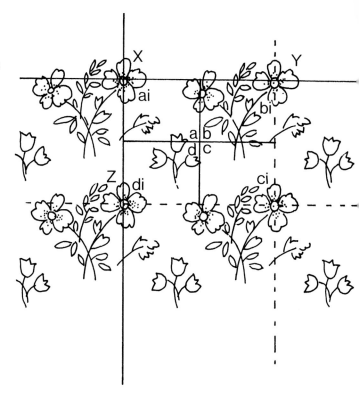

The first prerequisite for a good screenprinted fabric is a well-drawn design in accurate repeat. If the designer is incapable of doing the job himself it must be done in the studio and it needs great skill for a draughtsman, other than the designer, to re-create the *croquis* (or sketch design) as a completely accurate repeat. The kind of person who does this job well must not only be one who works with meticulous accuracy, but also one who is capable of appreciating any subtleties of personal drawing style which could so easily be altered and spoilt if understanding were lacking.

First draw a line joining two identical points on the design widthways, and one of them with an identical point lengthways also. If these points on the original repeat drawing are inaccurate and the lines do not therefore intersect at a right angle, adjustments will have to be made later. Then establish suitable repeat limits in both directions and mark these clearly on the drawing as shown.

On a fresh sheet of paper draw a new set of cross-lines and having cut the repeat into quarters, diagonally reverse the pieces and glue them down on the new sheet of paper. (It is important not to use water-based glue, or stretching will result.) Exactness of repeat is assured by this method because the parts of the repeat which must join are those which have been cut through – any slightly inaccurate areas are now in the centre and can be corrected fairly easily.

When preparing the tracings (known as 'sketches' or 'separations'), each colour in the design needs a separate sheet of Kodatrace or other transparent tracing film. In the centre of each sketch draw a repeat cross in Indian ink. Put

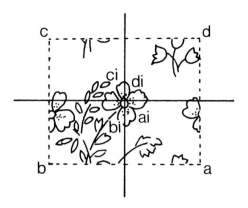

the other ends of these cross-lines in also. It is a good idea to start by outlining each of the colours in turn, after marking in the repeat crosses, and this is indeed essential where colours touch each other. Draw each tracing representing the separated colours on to the film with a photographic opaque paint such as Photopake or Klimsch Negropak. Painting must be done on the matt side of the film and it is advisable to powder the surface lightly with French chalk, in order to make sure that no grease is present.

Some firms work with such precision that the tracings are prepared 'line on line', that is without any 'allowance', or overlap, at all. To do this, of course, it is necessary for the draughtsman to be able to rely implicitly on the skill of the screenmakers and printers to match the accuracy in their respective jobs. If an allowance is necessary (and in screen printing it is usually a slight overlap to make the colours meet exactly on printing), this must be very finely calculated. The amount of the allowance is governed by all sorts of factors, such as type of cloth, range of dyestuff or pigment to be used, and the viscosity of the printpaste.

The foregoing description of the method of making a tracing applies to the bulk of designs prepared for screening, but if the drawing contains subtle tones and textures incapable of being copied opaquely directly on to the film, a variety of methods – such as pen lines and textures, stippling or sponges – are used to prepare each colour on a separate sheet of white paper. These separations are then each photographed through a cross-line screen to produce a positive. This positive has the tonal and textural areas now composed of fine but opaque dots.

Being able to use a cross-line screen to produce the positives for certain colour areas in a design helps to solve one set of problems, only to replace them with others. Most people will have noticed that when two layers of mesh are superimposed on each other a 'moiré' effect is produced; this can be seen at any window where terylene curtains are hung with a certain amount of fullness. This moiré effect also results if the cross-line screened positive is placed casually over the mesh of the screen fabric, and in order to avoid this, two important rules must be observed. First, there must be a size relationship between the count of the screen terylene and the count of the cross-line screen, and second, the screened positive must be placed over the sensitized screen at the angle which neutralizes the moiré effect.

There are obvious limits to the use of photomechanical screens when printing on cloth. Whereas on paper a fine count can be used, producing a great range of tone and so making the use of photogravure techniques worth while, on furnishing fabrics only about three or four tones are possible from the coarse meshes. A mesh count of 12 to 16 (used on fabric) allows 33 to 44 dots to the inch, and in lithographic work even 80 dots to the inch is considered coarse.

When the first attempts were made to neutralize the moiré effect the idea was adopted of stretching the screen fabric on to the frame at the required angle, instead of with the warp and weft being square to it. However, this was not only wasteful of fabric, but the resultant screen was not nearly so strong. Now the correct result is achieved by presenting the separation at the appropriate angle to the camera prior to photographing through the cross-line screen. (Photogravure work will be discussed again in Chapter 7 in connection with transfer printing, see p. 157.)

There are various ways of producing a number of repeats. In the case of designs of a fairly large scale and therefore, with not many repeats needed on the screen, several of these can be simply hand-painted on one film big enough to cover the screen. Designs of smaller scale needing many repeats on the screen can have the original hand-painted tracing photographically copied into negatives and then recopied as diapositives on special transparent paper as many times as are required to make up a larger positive, the necessary size for the screen. Contact copying boxes of various kinds and complexities are used for this purpose, as great care has to be taken to ensure the dimensional stability of the film, which has a tendency to stretch causing variation in size from repeat to repeat.

Various types of 'step-and-repeat' machines are also used, which can accommodate different sizes of screens, and which in a number of different ways enable all sizes of repeat to be transferred as many times as may be needed on to the sensitized screen surface or, of course, on to a full-size piece of film.

Stretching the screen

It is absolutely essential for all kinds of screen printing, whether hand or machine, to have a tightly stretched mesh. For this purpose, many types of stretcher are manufactured – from the simplest, but nevertheless effective, kinds made for small-scale use in colleges, to the much more elaborate ones used in large firms. The application of about 52 lb. pressure

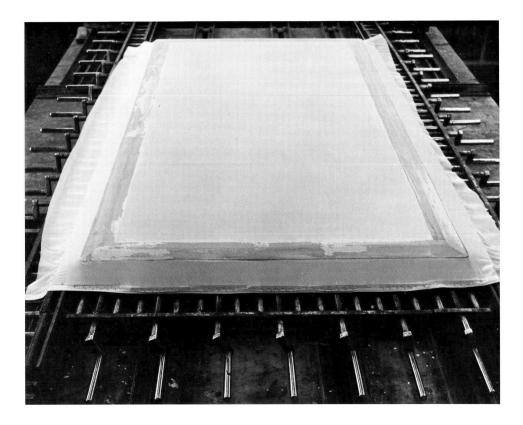

is necessary for a good result. As previously mentioned, bolting silk was, at first, widely used, then metal meshes of different types; latterly multifilament nylon and terylene have replaced these. Now it is being realized that monofilament meshes often give better printing results. The reason for this conclusion is that the printpaste tends to stick to the fibrous surface of a multifilament fabric, particularly where pigment colours are used. Printers find that a far longer time can be allowed to elapse between screen washings – again very important in pigment printing where colour build-up round the mesh can cause great variations both in the depth of colour and in the character of the printed fabric from one end of the print table to the other.

The screen fabric is fitted into the clamps of the stretcher, with the warp and weft accurately parallel to the sides of the screen frame. Non-metal gauze must be wetted out with a sponge and pre-stretched while still damp, before the final stretching is applied. (The extension of stabilized nylon gauze in both warp and weft direction should be about 6–10 per cent.)

When stretched, the fabric is fixed to the frame with special adhesive lacquer. Many lacquers are made for this purpose and the only essentials are that they must be resistant to heat and solvents and preferably take a short time to dry. When the adhesive layer is dry, and the screen taken out of

A screen being stretched in one type of stretching device. The fabric is pressed on to the pins with a brush or pad and the plates holding the pins are gradually tightened in sequence all round the frame until maximum tension is achieved. The adhesive is then painted on to the top surface of the screen-frame and left to dry.

Coating a flat screen with a light-sensitive emulsion: this should be done in a darkroom.

the stretcher, the resulting surplus gauze is fastened to the edges of the frame.

It is necessary to maintain an atmosphere which is free from moisture and dust. Often, in textile factories, this can be difficult, but it is nevertheless essential. If dust or fluff settles on the lacquer it can impair the sticking properties of the adhesive and if dust is allowed to reach the photolayer (which is to be applied next) while it is still 'tacky', pinholes will occur which have to be retouched.

Coating the screen

Before coating the gauze with the photolayer, it must be degreased. The light-sensitive emulsion, or photolayer, consisting of one of the polyvinyl alcohol products made specially for the purpose, is added to a solution of ammonium bichromate, the percentage varying in different recipes.

The emulsion may be applied with a flat, semi-soft brush. As the layer is not sensitive to light while still wet, the coating may be done in a diffused light, but bright daylight or strong artificial light must be avoided. The emulsion may also be applied with an angle or trough squeegee to the screen tilted at a slight angle. (At least two consecutive strokes of the squeegee across the screen are recommended.)

Metal angle squeegees can be used, but ones with coating edges of synthetic materials are better because too thin a layer is often applied with a metal edge.

Screens are then dried in a darkroom or cabinet immediately after coating. The drying temperature must not exceed 30° C. as a higher temperature would start to make the coating insoluble before exposure. After drying, the screen must be coated again, this time on the reverse side. Only subdued, or preferably yellow, light should be used, because the dry, coated side is of course now light-sensitive.

Exposing the screen

In the case of a single tracing, exposing the screen is simply a matter of putting the tracing in contact with the screen, now dried and coated on both sides, ensuring that firm contact is maintained by means of a glass plate or suction device, and exposing to light for about two to fifteen minutes (according to the type of tracing and exposing cabinet used).

When using several repeat diapositives, these must be mounted in accurate repeat on a colourless film. On this support film draw a grid to correspond to the various repeat squares needed. The diapositives, with the cross-marks on each one matched up to the grid on the clear support film, must then be fixed to it with adhesive tape. Then prepare black paper masks, suitably shaped to allow the diapositive assembly to be placed in contact with the sensitized screen without danger of light reaching any unwanted areas.

A light box suitable for college use.

If the assembly is not of the full screen size, then a copying machine or step-and-repeat machine must be used to expose the tracings the required number of times. The centre of the screen is marked and then the screen is placed in the machine with this centre mark matching the cross-mark on the glass plate. The repeat fittings are fixed on the guide rail by means of the measuring device provided. Outer limits are masked off with the previously cut black paper. With the room in darkness, or with yellow light only, contact is maintained with pressure boards or a vacuum pump, and the screen exposed for two to three minutes. Then move the copying carriage to the next register pin and repeat the process until all the repeats are completed. When the repeat is a 'half-drop' or 'step-half', as it is called in most textile factories the spare half repeat has to be specially masked off to make a straight selvedge line. There are now sophisticated step-and-repeat machines which can be programmed to repeat automatically.

Immediately after exposure to light the screen must be washed in warm water at about 55°–65° C. This washing clears all the unwanted photolayer from the unexposed parts of the mesh, and can best be done by placing the screen in a sink for a short while, and then spraying with warm

123

water. It is most important that this washing is done quickly – no more than three to four minutes being taken over it – as the exposed areas at this stage are extremely tender and may soften and peel off. After development the screens must be dried at a temperature again not exceeding 30° C.

Retouching and reinforcing the screen

Next examine the screen for faults or pinholes. If parts of the pattern area are clogged with photolayer, these must be damped and rubbed off gently with a soft brush, care being taken not to dislodge any of the developed layer. Pinholes are patched up with a resist paint. If for any reason the light exposure was a failure the whole photolayer can be removed by one of several different preparations according to the PVA colloid used in the coating.

To reinforce the lacquer coating, a trough or angle squeegee is used to coat the screen with a polyurethane reinforcing lacquer. This reinforcing has to be applied to both sides of the screen and then removed from the open areas either with a suction pump, if this is available, or if not with a cloth soaked in solvent; each side must be done separately and allowed to dry before the reverse side is coated.

The edges of the screen frame are reinforced by fixing adhesive tape round the inner edges of the frame and then coating them with screen lacquer. The screen is now ready for printing.

FLAT SCREEN PRINTING

Almost from the beginning of its development as an industry, screen printing, although in many factories entirely an exclusive hand process, was in others assisted to varying degrees by mechanical aids. These aids consisted of, for example, automatic printing tables, various means of screen lifting, assisted squeegees of different types and mechanized cloth movement.

Finally, in 1954, the first fully automatic flat-bed machine came into operation. This machine mechanized every single process, from the feeding-in of the cloth through gumming rollers, and the printing with varying numbers of squeegee movements, to the controlled lifting of cloth from the table and ending with passage into a drying cabinet. Basically, the operation of all flat-bed machines is the same, although in practice the solutions of the various problems involved in mechanized printing have been attempted in a number of interesting and ingenious ways. Holland, Switzerland, Austria and Italy have all contributed inventions and patents which are used in different machines, and it is interesting to compare the end products and see how each contributes something to the development of textile printing techniques.

The fabric, gummed to a backing, moves automatically the length of one repeat at a time. A battery of stationary screens, working in a line, drop down into the operative position, the squeegee presses the printpaste through the mesh of the screen which is then lifted, the cloth moves on one repeat and the process begins again.

In this country, the Swiss Buser machine and the Austrian Johannes Zimmer are probably the most widely used. The Buser is an extremely accurate machine using the conventional squeegee as a means of pressing the dye through the screen, while the Zimmer employs a completely novel and revolutionary 'magnet-roll' system which will be described in greater detail later in this section (see p. 129).

Hand screen printing.

The Buser flat-bed machine

This machine has a great reputation for accuracy and quality printing generally, although it is a sophisticated machine requiring extremely skilled and experienced operatives; given these, however, it is capable of producing fabric which is indistinguishable in quality from the best hand screen print. There are a number of special features incorporated in the machine which are interesting to note.

Each unit has a central adjusting device to hold the screens in the squeegee unit. These ensure quick and accurate fine setting and quick screen changing. If a narrow-width screen is being used it can be placed in a special unit with telescopic tubes. Each squeegee unit has its own motor and a two-speed gearing provides for two squeegee speeds of 640 mm. and 922 mm. per second (approximately 25 in. and 36 in. per second). The centrifugal brake of this squeegee unit ensures soft starting and accurate stopping, and the number of strokes and the pressure can be individually adjusted for each unit, although obviously the speed of the whole machine has to be geared to the speed of the unit taking the most strokes. 1, 2 or 4 squeegee strokes can be arranged; the desirable number is a matter for experience and is influenced by the character of the design, the quality of cloth and the viscosity of the printpaste.

In the early 1970s a '*flood stroke*' *operation* was introduced. This is a single stroke made with the screen raised from the table. The stroke fills the gauze openings with printpaste and after lowering the screens to cloth level the usual squeegee stroke is made. Thus, in the time of a single stroke almost double the quantity of printpaste is applied to the cloth. With this operation it is possible to increase output in all cases where a single stroke is not sufficient. Other advantages of this procedure are sharper contours and the avoidance of bubbling, because there is no

The Swiss Buser flat-bed machine showing cloth entering and being gummed down at the left; the screen units along a horizontal bed; and the printed cloth being separated from the blanket and passing into the drier, while the blanket goes back underneath to be washed and dried ready to repeat the cycle.

Two Liberty Tana lawns: examples of twentieth-century engraved roller printing.

Simple Solar: a hand screen print by Shirley Craven, 1967.

air to get rid of. After printing the screen can, if it is desirable, be lifted off at an angle; this may be necessary when a lot of colour has been applied to a delicate fabric, to prevent the cloth becoming detached from the screen when it is lifted off.

The machine can be fitted with a *thermoplastic glueing device* as well as one of the conventional variety. This method dispenses with the need for a back-grey and is suitable, and indeed highly successful, for most fabrics – even those of comparative fineness and transparency. As the glue is made adhesive only when heat is applied, the use of a conventional glue on the top is not precluded. (For a description of the method of application see the section on rotary screen printing, p. 150.)

Since the early 1970s there has been a vast increase in the yardage of knitted fabric being printed, and because of its elasticity this can present problems which are difficult to overcome. It has been found that the method used in the Buser flat-bed machine to feed the cloth in without tension, and also the tensionless release of the damp, printed fabric from the printing blanket and its transport in this state into the drier, ensure a good, accurately fitting print unspoilt by distortions.

The Buser flat-bed machines differ from others in their continuous running of the belt in the vertical feed-in unit and also on the underside of the machine. The belt is kept in continuous movement on the underside of the printing table, on one side of the feed-in unit, by an electric motor with gearing. Compensation between intermittent and continuously running belt sections is provided by floating belt drums. This continuous and tension-free passage of the cloth on to the belt allows for even gumming and an even, thorough washing of the belt.

In the printing section, clamping magnets, arranged along the sides of the table top over the whole machine length, grip the belt and advance it one repeat hydraulically. During printing, the belt is clamped fast and at the same time the advance magnets are released and returned to the starting position. The speed the machine is run at can vary a great deal. A firm requiring the best quality out of the machine, rather than greater output, will run it at about 300 yards an hour only, but it can be run at much higher speeds if desired.

The Johannes Zimmer flat-bed machine

The Zimmer flat-bed machines have, as I mentioned, a special feature known as a '*magnet-roll*' *system* for pressing the colour through the mesh of the screen. This device is a simple, round metal roller varying in diameter from 3 mm. to 18 mm., which is placed loosely in the screen with the printpaste and which is moved along by means of magnet coils under the printing blanket, which draw the printpaste through the gauze.

(*Opposite, above*) Examples of fabric printed by the 'Star transfer' process, 1953.

(*Opposite, below*) Examples of polychromatic dyeing (*centre*) and transfer printing, 1972.

The Swiss Buser flat-bed machine showing the central adjusting device which holds the screens in the squeegee units, and ensures quick and accurate fine setting and quick changing of screens. Narrow screens which do not occupy the full width of the print table can be used in conjunction with telescopic tubes.

(*Right*) Printing in operation on the Johannes Zimmer flat-bed machine. Note the downward movement of the 'magnet roll' system of pressing the colour through the cloth. The fine steel rod can just be seen passing over the pattern area, drawing a thin film of colour with it. The colour is fed from the trough directly on to the screen through fine holes which ensure a small, regular supply.

The other main difference to note is that whereas the conventional squeegees used in other machines operate from selvedge to selvedge across the fabric, the magnet-roll squeegee works down the cloth, at right angles to the selvedge. There are a number of advantages claimed for this invention, possibly one of the most important being that no uneven wear takes place on the rods – as can occur with a blade-type squeegee. As for the downwards movement, this is quite an advantage at the present time when there are so many fabrics of greatly increased width coming on to the market, because it takes no longer to print an excessively wide cloth than it does to print a narrow one. A high rate of production can be maintained because many fabrics can be satisfactorily printed by a single stroke of the rod.

ROTARY SCREEN PRINTING

The latest development in the screenprinting side of the textile industry is its adoption of the rotary principle. Although rotary screenprinting machines have been in commercial use since as far back as 1954, it is only since the middle of the 1960s that they have really gained in popularity in Britain. One of the latest and most interesting models is the wide-width machine made by Peter Zimmer/Kufstein for the printing of sheets and bedspreads.

There is little doubt that in the next few years rotary screen printing will gain an even bigger share of the market than it has already. This increasing share will be taken over mostly from the engraved roller printer, but also from the flat screen side. Constant refinements in rotary screen-making techniques and new developments in the printing machines themselves are making it possible for screen printing to be used in an ever-increasing number of different fields where a short while ago it would have been impossible, or so difficult as to be dismissed out of hand. For instance, pile carpets and complete bedspreads can now be screen-printed and rotary screens are used in photogravure transfer printing. Even from this it can be seen to be an extremely flexible method of printing and one capable of a variety of developments – and in fact screen printing and making, from being a very simple process, is quickly becoming a sophisticated art. Peter Zimmer, one of the pioneers in the rotary field, is convinced that it is a method which embodies all the good points of flat screen and roller printing, with none of the disadvantages, and even allowing for the natural enthusiasm of the inventor, many of the advantages are self-evident. This does not mean, though, that it in any way invalidates the use of the engraved roller printer for many jobs in the future.

The latest rotary machines were created specifically to meet the modern need of shorter set-up times and are highly economic with short print orders of 2,000 yards or so per colourway (each different colouring of the same design) as well as being efficient and reasonably cheap for longer runs and short or long repeat orders. Because of this economic printing of comparatively short yardages, combined with the versatility and freedom of design interpretation associated with screen printing, it may go some way towards bringing a better and more adventurous quality into the mass-market side of the industry. If converters are able to show a profit without having to print very big yardages, while at the same time knowing that it is also economic to repeat with larger orders when these are forthcoming, this may give them that extra incentive to chance designs that are not quite so 'safe'. In any case the market is tending much more towards swifter fashion changes, and therefore automatically to less yardage per design. Whereas before the last war production was talked of in terms of 'lumps' (i.e. 120 yards), it is now referred to in yards only, 5,000 yards being a good order instead of 5,000 lumps.

One of the unfortunate features of design since the introduction of machinery, particularly in England, has been the seemingly widening gap between the design standards of the manual and mechanized sides of the textile industry. Although there is nothing in the roller-printing method to prevent good prints – rather the reverse in fact, because accurate printing of fine detail is a feature of the process only too well demonstrated by many of the nineteenth-century examples and also by the Liberty Tana Lawn Paisleys and other intricate designs roller-printed nowadays – nevertheless, the assumption in some areas of the mass-production industry has nearly always been that cheaply priced cloth could have anything put on it. As a result, people have almost lost the natural taste and sense of pattern and colour that must have been inherent when they were making patchwork quilts and samplers.

Block printing had virtually ceased by the end of the last century except for the printing of expensive silk and fine wools for an exclusive market – the speedier Perrotine did not catch on in England. Hand screen work provided couture fabrics and avant-garde furnishings in the 1940s and 1950s with designs whose ideas gradually, very gradually, filtered down the market. It is of course quite right, and indeed highly desirable, that there should be small experimental ranges (for however the industrialist may criticize the prestige value of these low-profit-making and possibly even unprofitable fabrics, the mass market very much needs the ideas and colour forecasts they provide). It is a pity if cheaper goods get second best, but perhaps with widened education helped by the rotary screen machines, the two sides may draw closer together. This bringing together has been started by flat screen printing machines, although most of their work has come from the now almost completely obsolescent hand screen trade.

As far as England was concerned, the period after the Second World War was a tricky one for the Lancashire cotton trade, for although there was a great revival of interest in British design, with the Britain Can Make It and Festival of Britain exhibitions, and with collections of hand-screened fabrics such as those from Heal's and Edinburgh Weavers beginning to give Britain a name for design, the fate of the mass market was not so good. Many printworks had to close down and the rest had to be radically restructured in order to survive the influx of cheap, and often well-printed, cotton from Hong Kong, and were being dragged down even further by the need to occupy the hundreds of roller printing machines with which the printworks were equipped.

It has been calculated that in the early 1950s, there were about a thousand roller machines in Britain; now only about seventy are in operation. This unfortunate situation, in which far too much mass-production machinery was available for a shrinking market, was probably a reason for the lack of interest in rotary screen machines in this country, and for the concentration on the flat screen types when new machinery was contemplated. For although they are now proving very versatile, in the 1950s firms would fight shy of any innovation that seemed geared to fairly large-scale production, even if it held a promise of economic shorter runs as well.

In any event, it is surprising that in the 1950s, when developments in both flat and rotary screen techniques were well under way (Peter Zimmer/Kufstein had a prototype rotary machine in 1955) and were apparently running fairly level, the flat screen side should suddenly be pushed so far ahead that in the 1954–64 period about ten different versions of the machine were made; but until the Hanover Trade Fair of 1964, the Aljaba was the only rotary system in commercial use. This is strange, particularly when one realizes that automatic flat screen techniques are in a way a step backwards, as continuity of printing – an important feature of roller printing – is lost.

One reason for the ability of the automatic flat screen machines to develop apace, was that any speed-up was one of simply mechanizing what had already been fully exploited by hand screen printing. Flat screenmaking techniques were already perfected and thoroughly understood – no new inventions were really required – whereas for the rotary method to progress, new approaches to several problems were necessary.

The Aljaba rotary machine

In his logical analysis of the difficulties besetting the development of rotary screen printing, A.J.C. de O. Barros, the inventor of the Aljaba machine, sees two features of prime importance: the method of applying the printpaste, and the fabric of the screen itself. Once these two major aspects had been satisfactorily dealt with, the actual rotary mechanisms used to create the final printing machine would follow existing ideas.

Only one method of applying printpaste was universally used with the flat screen up to the 1950s: the flat-bladed squeegee we have seen already. Most of the experiments in the rotary field used this type, and all patents taken out from the 1930s onwards were concerned only with the blade applicators. However, Barros found that certain drawbacks

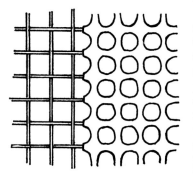

Diagram illustrating the effect of electro-deposition on the woven metal gauze.

were present with the squeegee. Being flat and in a fixed position it tended to work against the rotary action of the machine, causing strain which resulted in damage and distortion, or even stoppage of the machine altogether. This was particularly so when printing heavy fabrics. Also, when fine-edged squeegees were used they wore down quickly, but coarsening the edge only resulted in a loss of sharp outlines.

To resolve this problem Barros designed 'a metallic roller device with a freely rotating motion and running at a tangent to the inner surface of the screen'. This method was strong, equally suitable (with changes of diameter) for all types of fabric, and did not damage the screen (see also, on p. 129, the Johannes Zimmer flat-bed machine, developed at this time). In 1954–55, when the Aljaba machine was first made a commercial proposition, rubber squeegee blades were not proving feasible, but by 1964 this method had been redeveloped and is used in several of the later rotary screen-printing machines, such as the Stork and Buser machines which will be discussed later in this chapter (see p. 139).

The other major problem was the design and construction of the rotary screen itself. Many different gauzes have been used at various times in the making of flat screens for both hand and mechanical screen printing such as: bolting silk, multi- and monofilament nylon and terylene, phosphor-bronze, monel metal and stainless steel. But even the strongest metal meshes are in themselves not strong enough for a cylinder screen and so either they must be strengthened in some way, or the screen should be a continuous metal cylinder which is finely perforated all over (this is the idea developed by Stork, which will be discussed later). Not only must the metal gauze be strong, but the wires must not be too thick nor the openings too small, for both these factors would work against the strength needed for a good cylinder screen.

After various experiments, Barros found that for best results the wire should be 0·008 in., the mesh opening 0·003 in. and the free printing surface 19 per cent. This is not commercially practicable and so electro-deposition had to be used. Finally, phosphor-bronze and monel metal gauzes of 100-mesh 42 s.w.g. were chosen and electroplated with copper to bring them to the required thickness. After copper-plating, the gauze was 'flashed' with nickel to protect it from oxidization.

At first two types of screen were obtained by this method: one was an all-metal screen and the other was reinforced by coating with protective lacquer, as in flat screen work. Barros describes the two types in the following way:

To prepare the first type, while the screen was still in its flat form, the design was engraved photographically by coating with a photosensitive emulsion and exposure to light. This coating was treated with graphite to make it

electrically conducting and then the screen was plated by
the method previously described [see p. 134]. The parts
covered with the photosensitive emulsion were found to
have a protective film of copper and in the open areas of
the design the wires were thickened to the extent required.
[See also the galvano method, p. 143.]

For the second type, the screen, while still flat, was
submitted to the same plating process and then photo-
engraved, after which the protective coating was applied
in the usual manner, giving a screen covered with
lacquer.

Both types of screen were then made circular with the
aid of a mandrel, the screen being cut in accordance with
the configuration of the design, so that it could be soldered
into a cylinder. The minimum space required for the
passage of the soldered join is about 3 mm. (0·118 in.), which
in most designs is readily available.

These types of screen were used in the first Aljaba rotary
screenprinting machines marketed in 1954.

While these experiments were being carried out, flat
screen machines were developing rapidly, and gaining many
outlets. Nylon and terylene gauzes were beginning to be
used and Barros felt that advantage could be taken of these
new fabrics, to do away with the obvious drawback of
having to use electroplated metallic gauzes.

The two-ply screen

The outcome of these experiments was the two-ply screen,
consisting of a metal mesh support screen and a nylon or
terylene engraved screen, used today. The support screen
could now be designed solely to give strength and maximum
resistance to wear and tear. It also controls printpaste flow
and distribution. The big advantage of this system is that in
theory it can be made as efficient as possible for these purposes
without reference to the kind of design to be printed, or the
cloth to be printed on.

For this support screen a continuous metal mesh is needed
and it is made in the following way. The woven gauze is
cut to the appropriate size and both edges are specially
prepared. The metal fabric is then formed into a cylindrical
shape and the two edges are abutted together and welded
with a ribbon of brazing alloy. 'Seaming', as this process is
called, is done by machine, but nevertheless requires a high
degree of skill on the part of the operator. After seaming,
mounting rings are soldered into each end of the wire mesh
cylinder. The cylinder is then flashed with a light nickel
deposit which increases its rigidity and also protects the
phosphor-bronze wires from discoloration on contact with
printpaste. (It is possible now to make a stabilized weave
which is durable enough to be able to dispense with the
nickel deposit.)

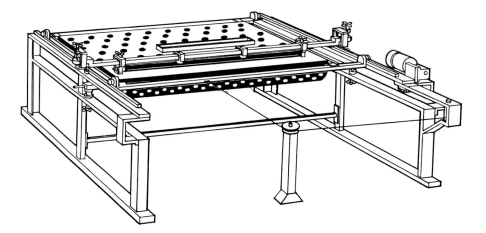

The Aljaba screen-transfer apparatus. The flat screen engraved with a 'negative film' can be seen on top of the rotary screen receiving the pattern in positive form.

Just as the support screen can be designed in the best possible way for its particular job, so the engraver is now free to use the type of screen fabric he considers best for each design or part of a design: nylon, terylene, or even metal. The support screen (or 'base screen') has a terylene, or other fabric, sleeve fitted over it and heavy metal collars pushed into position at each end of the stretching machine. The ends of the tubular fabric are bonded to the base screen by means of an adhesive, to a depth of about four inches.

The mesh count of the base screen is normally between 60 and 65 threads to the inch for Duplex printing (both sides of the cloth), though the Aljaba system is the only one as yet which is adapted to Duplex. A more open mesh can be used for Simplex (single-sided) printing. The mesh of the polyester, or other cover, is determined by the character and fineness of the design to be printed. Mesh counts vary from 100 to 250 warp threads per inch and of course are selected to suit the design and the cloth to be printed on.

The design is transferred to the two-ply screens by a simple method whereby a conventional flat screen is photographically engraved with a 'negative film', then used to print the design on to an Aljaba two-ply cylindrical screen coated with a special lacquer. The flat screen and the cylinder to be patterned are placed together in a specially designed transfer-frame. In this frame the flat screen moves horizontally a distance equal to the circumference of the rotary screen, or slightly more, according to how the design separations have been prepared. While the flat screen moves horizontally, the rotary one rotates on an axle fixed to the frame of the transfer apparatus (see diagram).

As the flat screen used for transferring the design is not itself reinforced with screen lacquer, the design may be removed with chemicals and the screen used for other designs. The two-ply screens made in this way are long-lasting and when the pattern is finished with, the tubular screen fabric may be removed and the support screen re-covered with a new tube of nylon or terylene. The fact that both flat screens and base screens can be re-used in this way

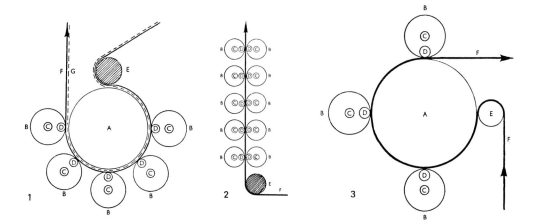

is a great advantage from the point of view of cost, while the very using of a flat screen for engraving purposes in itself means that little in the way of screenmaking technique has to be newly learnt. But in practice, although it is a simple process to engrave the screens, in some cases they have to be remade because of a tendency to separate from the base or support screen.

Simplex machines

In the Simplex machines, for single-sided printing, the rotary screens are placed close together round a central pressure bowl, and the fabric is firmly supported so that many different types of fabric can be printed with reasonably accurate registration. It is possible to convert uneconomic engraved roller printing machines by replacing the roller printing machine head at a fairly low cost, and this has been done in a number of machines.

A printpaste of very high viscosity is used in Aljaba machines and it is fed through PVC tubing by means of an automatically controlled colour pump. As we have seen, a stainless steel roller squeegee is used to press the colour through the mesh, and by changing the size and type of roller squeegee thick or thin fabrics can be printed. In practice, though, as with the Zimmer machines which also use a metal roller for this purpose, the experienced printer usually finds that he does not get as much variation in result from the different widths of rod as is sometimes claimed, and so he restricts his use to a small number. Colour sequence is from dark to light as in other screen machines, rather than light to dark as for engraved roller work, to avoid smearing (see p. 72).

Because of the absence of external doctor blades and colour-boxes, the screens themselves may be arranged to operate in the position most convenient to the fabric and process, for example above or below a fabric running horizontally, against a fabric running vertically, or round a central pressure cylinder (see comparative diagrams).

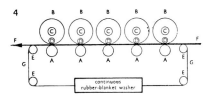

(1) Typical arrangement for single-face (Simplex) printing machine: A pressure bowl; B screen; C axle (including printpaste feed); D roller squeegee; E guide roller; F fabric; G back-grey or continuous blanket.
(2) Three-colour flock printing machine.
(3) Arrangement for double-face (Duplex) printing machine.
(4) Five-colour blanket printing machine.

Ten-colour Aljaba Duplex machine. Note the simple vertical arrangement of screens.

The Aljaba Duplex machine

The screens operate vertically in pairs in this machine – the most convenient arrangement for Duplex printing. The squeegee inside the screen acts as a pressure roller for the screen that partners it, and so, not surprisingly, the Duplex machine is not only simple in construction, but is also relatively inexpensive.

The registration of the pairs of screens is controlled by adjusting the fit of the front cylinder screen, again making the operation of the machine fairly easy. But, on the other hand, remember that the cloth is not supported from one pair of screens to the next and so one cannot expect to get close registration, or to be able to use any but the heaviest and most stable of cloths. Within these limits, the work is of reasonable quality and certainly the two sides match each other, shape for shape and line for line, far better than the old Duplex, where one side of the cloth was printed and then it passed over another pressure bowl in an 'S' bend to be similarly printed on its underside. Incidentally, engraving pairs of screens presents few problems, as one is printed from the top surface of the flat screen and the second from the bottom – resulting in the required mirror image.

The Aljaba Duplex machines can print at the rate of about 30–40 yards a minute, but could operate considerably faster if speedier drying could be managed. Duplex printing by this method deposits a great deal of printpaste on the cloth, and as mentioned, it is of a much higher viscosity than for any other method. Very careful drying is needed, to avoid 'marking off' and the fabric must not be allowed to touch anything until it is almost completely dry. The thicker paste also prevents damage to cloth from leakage when the machine is stationary, and makes for sharper outline printing.

But for the really cheap end of the market it is sometimes too expensive a method – and certainly when pigment colours are used it leaves the cloth extremely stiff.

If the Duplex machine is needed at any time for single-sided work, this can be carried out by printing against an empty rear screen, or preferably by replacing the rear screen with a rubber roller. Only fabrics with good dimensional stability are considered suitable for printing either way on the Duplex machine. It is claimed that under normal conditions an eight-colour Simplex design can be changed within thirty minutes. As for the Duplex machine, the claim is one and a quarter hours for an eight-colour job.

Certainly as far as Duplex work is concerned, Aljaba machines do, in most cases, produce a better job than the Duplex engraved roller machines, though in single-side work one does not get the variety and fineness of detail possible with other rotary screen systems. In fact it is in the field of Duplex printing that the Aljaba system has been most widely used in England. In other parts of the world 'double-sided fabrics' have never been popular, whereas in this country Duplex curtaining printed by engraved rollers has for many years occupied a place in the cheap end of the market (the machine was first used in 1875). The designs were always printed on poor-quality cloth and almost always, in recent years, contain fairly big areas of black or other dark texture – a device used to cover up inaccurate matching of pattern on the two sides, and other faults. However, the Aljaba Duplex machine has, without a doubt, brought about a great change in the character of Duplex designs, which are now much more clean and bright in colour and have a much greater variety of style.

The Stork rotary machine

As noted in the last section, although a number of different people in different places in the early 1950s were concerning themselves with experiments in rotary screen printing, only Aljaba machines were in commercial use up to the mid-1960s. It was not until 1963 that Stork of Amsterdam succeeded, after a long period of research, in producing seamless cylinder screens suitable for textile printing; these were of the finely perforated sieve-like variety, not woven mesh

The latest Stork rotary machine showing the automatic colour-feed system.

ones as in the Aljaba machines. Peter Zimmer/Kufstein were also working on this type and as with many ideas, development was almost simultaneous. It gave a tremendous boost to the screenprinting industry, opening up its use to a much wider field. The possibility of now being able to use screenmaking techniques and styles of design for bigger yardages gave it great appeal, as did its simpler operation, needing less skilled workers than rotary machines offered by the longer-established roller printers.

Stork also managed successfully to solve the difficulties besetting the use of a squeegee applicator for the printpaste, and so in 1963–64, when the Stork rotary machine was first used commercially, it contained the two different solutions to Barros's two stated problems mentioned on p. 133. It was closely followed by other firms such as Zimmer and Buser, all of whom introduced subtle variants into their designs. However, while some machines employ squeegees and others metal rods, none use woven wire screens except the Aljaba.

Relative merits of rotary screen

As far as Stork are concerned, they are so confident of the continuing success of rotary screen printing that in 1969 they discontinued production of the flat-bed type altogether. But from the printer's point of view, opinions are a little divided as to the relative merits of engraved roller, rotary screen or flat screen machines. While most authorities are agreed that the newest flat and rotary machines are good, well designed and capable of doing extremely satisfactory work, the reasons for using rotary screen as opposed to roller printing are determined by a number of factors, not necessarily entirely connected with the machines themselves.

Broadly speaking, established printworks with the necessary skills for engraved roller printing machines, are happy to carry on using them and are full of praise for the standard of work these machines produce. And although it is true that roller printing machines are in most cases uneconomic for smaller yardages, nevertheless, within large organizations where it is necessary to print for the different firms within the group as well as for outside customers, terms can be arranged to make the printing of even 500 to 1,000 yards per colour a workable proposition. This is obviously better than bulk printing, expensive warehousing, and the possible selling-off of unwanted cloth. So, although some rotary printing machines may start to take over from the older machines it will be some time before the majority are replaced.

On the other hand, the rotary printer is noted for not needing inherited skills and long training; this is a decided incentive to those firms already established as good-quality hand and flat screen printers who want to increase their output of cloth, and also it is a source of attraction for energetic people with capital but little or no textile experience to build up a printworks from scratch. Some smaller firms, too, find that they can get by without using skilled union labour.

As far as roller printing is concerned, its two main disadvantages are the inability to produce yardages of less than 10,000 per design economically (except in certain specialized circumstances), and the disproportionately long 'down' time, that is the time required for setting up the machine, changing the colours and pitching the rollers. The copper cylinders are heavy and unwieldy, making changes extremely slow. The pitching speed is 10 yards per minute and a lot of 'seconds' result before the design is in fit. A single-colour machine may produce 125 yards a minute but a multicolour printer can manage only about 60 yards for a four-colour job, while the rotary screen machine is capable of reaching 100 yards per minute for six colours, provided the design does not have a great deal of close fitting. (And here you have also a very important point of comparison: nothing as yet in rotary work can beat the exactness of fit and fineness of detail of engraved roller printing – and this achieved at a fair speed.)

One other disadvantage of roller printing is loss of colour brilliance due to the great pressure required to get the printpaste out of the engraving – about 400 lb., even in the newer machines, and as much as 3 tons in some old ones. This loss of brightness can also result from pick-up of colour from roller to roller. The tendency to smear is the main reason that printing is from light to dark in engraved roller work. All screen work produces cleaner, brighter colours. Another irritation is the width restriction. Latterly, cloth is being made in a much greater variety of widths and so more and more this is being seen as a disadvantage. But probably the one feature which will eventually make for a change-over to rotary machines is the fact that a long training coupled with experience, is necessary for roller printing: the machines are not easy to supervise, employ difficult printing techniques, and have a high accident risk if insufficient training is given.

When rotary printers were first developed, the aim was to combine the good points from the two methods: speed, continuity and quick and continuous registration from engraved roller work, and from flat screen techniques the great advantage of lack of pressure (resulting in surface colour which is clean, bright and uncrushed), the possibility of large repeats, and as previously mentioned, short set-up times and the economic printing of smaller yardages. As yet the old engraving machines, although often eighty or ninety years old, are in fine working order, but when replacements are felt to be necessary for any reason they will almost certainly be rotary screen.

Making the rotary screen

It is possible to purchase the rotary screens from a manufacturer, such as Stork or Buser, and then simply to engrave them in the conventional manner. These consist of seamless cylinders regularly perforated over the whole surface and made of pure nickel. The screen walls are very thin – between 0·08 and 0·19 mm. In spite of this apparent fragility the life of the screens is claimed to be quite long provided they are handled carefully and according to instructions; indeed there are some that have printed a million yards without breakage. The big advantage of using this type of nickel screen is that, having purchased the base screen, any firm with knowledge of flat screen engraving techniques can adapt themselves easily and without excessive expenditure to the engraving of the rotary type.

The base screens so purchased are usually made on a deeply engraved solid cylindrical matrix. The engraving is produced by mill engraving or by an electronic technique. A hexagonal mesh form is nearly always used for rotary screens because this shape gives the maximum openness. This is sometimes expressed as an air:metal or hole:land ratio. The deeply engraved cells must be filled with an insulator before the matrix is immersed in the nickel bath. The nickel is deposited on the 'land', and although it grows outwards it does also spread sideways, partially closing the holes. It follows therefore that the resulting screen ends up with a different hole:land ratio from the one on the matrix. This ratio is vitally important for the resulting printed fabric. If, however, an electroplating unit is available (as for instance at a roller engraving works, where this process is used to give a plating of chromium as a protection to the engraved copper cylinder), then it is probably advantageous to set up a section for making the screens themselves on the premises or to employ the technique of direct galvanic design (GDD). Peter Zimmer's own explanation of the various methods is to the following effect:

(*Above*) Part of a rotary screen enlarged to show the hexagonal mesh formation.

(*Left*) A rotary screen of the Stork type with the pattern engraved upon it, showing the sieve-like character of the metal mesh.

Whether the aim is to produce:

(*a*) a perforated sleeve,

(*b*) a thin cylinder, or

(*c*) a screen designed during manufacture (i.e. the galvano type),

the application of the nickel is nearly always the same. A cylindrical matrix (often of stainless steel), the necessary circumference and length, is made the cathode in an electrical circuit. Nickel in molecular form moves from the nickel anodes in the galvanic bath through the electrolyte to the matrix and forms a deposit. So a plain nickel cylinder is formed, the wall thickness depending on the

intensity of the current applied – textile screens are 0·08
0·10 mm (0·003–0·004 in.) or sometimes a little thicker.

If, however, an insulator is applied to areas of the
matrix (i.e. in the form of a patterned mesh), the nickel
will not adhere and in these areas are formed holes which
later permit colour to be pressed through to the cloth.

(a) The holes can be uniformly distributed as a regular
mesh (rather as the apertures in a woven fabric would be),
and then a photo-lacquer applied and the screen developed
in the normal way.

(b) With etched screens this insulation is reached by
applying the photo-sensitive layer and a patterned screen
film on to the thin nickel cylinder (which later forms the
screen) and exposing and developing. The etching acid will
then only affect the metal at places where no insulation
remains.

(c) The direct galvano technique (GDD) is a blending
together of the two former methods – the matrix is coated
with a photo-layer on which a screened film is exposed.
The resulting insulating areas which resist the nickel
deposit are the designed screen.

The most difficult part in the making of rotary screens is
the withdrawal of the screen from the matrix (or 'forming-
sleeve'). When a solid matrix is used, various means can be
adopted to facilitate this, but it is still tricky. For instance,
chromic acid over the matrix very slightly oxidizes the
surface, making it passive and so more likely to ease the
screen withdrawal. The solid matrices have steel end-collars
which are used to give electrical contact in the plating tank;
the coating is controlled automatically, and provided the
matrix was absolutely free from dirt or grease, the nickel-
coated screen can be removed by hand. If, however, there
was even a tiny particle of dust on the surface, a lesion will
have resulted which will need to be forcibly broken by
gripping the screen with pincers.

An answer to this problem has been developed by Peter
Zimmer in the form of an elastic matrix. This is a thin metal
cylinder which is flexible and can be altered in circumference by about 1 mm. by stretching. The fact that it is
light in weight, 6–20 lb., as compared with the usual 500–
1,000 lb., is also a big advantage. The principle behind the
method is the expansion and contraction of the thin nickel
matrix, effected by means of an inflatable rubber roller.

First, the thin nickel sleeve (or elastic matrix) is drawn
over an inflatable rubber roller, which is then inflated. The
nickel is coated with a photosensitive lacquer and the rubber
roller is then deflated. Next, a full-size screened positive
(photographed through screens giving hexagonal dots) is
fixed round the nickel with an overlap of about 0·5 mm.
and carefully fastened. The rubber is then inflated a little,
so bringing the edges into a position where they just touch
each other; this ensures a very good join. Next, the screen is

exposed. Afterwards the film is removed and the screen developed. The rubber is again deflated, and the nickel sleeve complete with its pattern in hardened photo-layer is slid off and placed in the nickel-plating bath. On completion of the plating the sleeve is again drawn over the rubber roller. First it is inflated to slightly stretch the nickel sleeve and then immediately deflated, so releasing the galvano screen from the matrix, enabling its completely easy removal. In this way a galvano directly designed screen (GDD) is produced.

At first it was found that the rubber tended to pinhole and burst, but this difficulty has now been overcome. These galvano screens are durable and much favoured by Peter Zimmer/Kufstein for use in their rotary machines, although the more easily produced, conventionally engraved nickel screens are equally usable in them too. It must be realized that the galvano method is not one to be adopted by any and every firm which has a screenmaking department. Not only are the specialized skills of experienced platers required, but the facilities for ensuring a completely clean atmosphere, and maintaining this, are essential. The cost of setting up and maintaining a good department is great, particularly if there is not sufficient work to keep it regularly employed. Another important point with regard to small-scale operating difficulties is that constant skilled surveillance of the plating tanks must be kept up, whether they are in use or not, because if any foreign matter gets into the fluid, the whole, costing hundreds of pounds, will have to be destroyed. When a new tank is prepared it has to be 'worked in' until the plating becomes consistent and the correct timings can be worked out. Therefore, a firm setting up a galvano section needs to be sure of a constant flow of work – either their own or commissioned for other people.

Engraving nickel cylinder screens

The nickel screens are packed flat in a special way to ensure safe delivery. When required for use, they are put in a heat cabinet in order to bring them back to a cylindrical shape. A clamp is then placed inside the cylinder and gradually sprung out to the correct size. Before coating, the screen must be thoroughly cleaned and degreased. Usually this can be done with a nylon brush in a solution of saturated chromic acid; this is washed off with water and the screen then treated with 20 per cent soda ash; it is washed again, and finally dried in a dust-free place.

To coat the screen, various types of light-sensitive emulsion can be used – some, such as EWD 1040, which need a hardener, and others, such as Stork CL-50, which do not. Emulsions have to be carefully chosen with reference to such things as amount of wear, type of fabric to be printed, and in particular the class of dyestuff or pigment to be used. This last is of prime importance, as certain chemicals and solvents tend to break down emulsions very quickly. The

Stork screens are packed flat in a special way to ensure safe delivery. When required for use, they are put in a heat cabinet to regain their circular shape.

(*Above*) Stork screens restored to the correct size and circular shape are ready, after degreasing, to be coated with photographic emulsion.

(*Above, right*) The mechanical coating of a rotary screen.

screen is coated with a specially designed circular squeegee or doctor which is moved upwards. Three or four coats are applied, with short drying periods in between. This is done in a box suitable for the purpose at temperatures of about 77°–86° F. If the screen is not to be used immediately it must be stored at a constant temperature in a refrigerator. This prevents any premature polymerization of the emulsion.

When ready to expose, the screen is placed in a copying machine. This consists of a driving shaft, or mandrel, which rotates and which carries an inflatable rubber sleeve. Over this the rotary screen is placed, and the sleeve inflated until it exactly fits the inside circumference of the cylinder. Behind this is the light source (a series of fluorescent tubes arranged in a semicircle in a mobile sheet-steel frame), and when a positive the full size of the screen is available it is necessary only to switch on the timer which controls the exposure time and to set the shaft rotating. When part-films are to be used, however, the screen has to be provided with repeat marks corresponding to the size of the film. This is done with a special ruling device, which has metal arms, each bearing a ruling point. These can be regulated to the required distances and used to mark off the screen. In practice, carbon paper is sometimes needed to give extra depth to the mark. The positive is then fitted in position and the other areas blacked

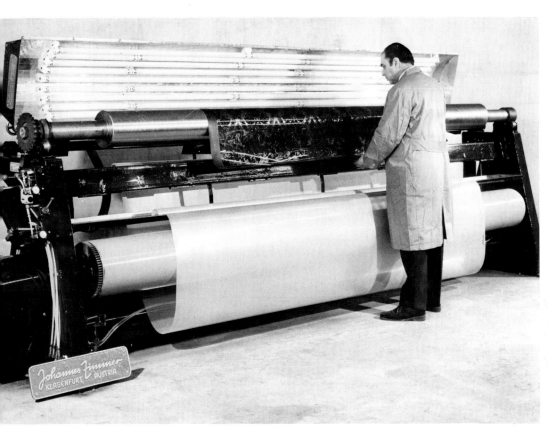

out. The shutter is opened to allow the light through and the screen rotates for a controlled amount of time. It is extremely important that the temperature does not get too high as this would polymerize the non-exposed parts of the screen and make them less soluble in water. It follows that not too many separate repeats can be used. Usually high-pressure mercury tubes are the best light source and a good forced-air-draught cooling system is necessary to prevent the film sticking to the emulsion and to avoid damage to the inflatable sleeve.

After exposure, the screen is removed from the sleeve and immersed in water at 50°–77° F. for about fifteen minutes or so, with several changes of water. Proper support must be provided at both sides, and developing and washing stands are made with lights so placed as to make continuous inspection an easy matter. If the exposure time and other factors are correct, the non-exposed parts will wash off easily when hosed down. The rotary screen is then placed on a shaft in the inspection stand and touched up if needed. If the emulsion is one which requires a hardener, it is applied at this stage with a circular squeegee, and the surplus sucked out by vacuum. When dry, the emulsion coating must be baked (or 'cured') in a polymerizing cabinet at temperatures up to 200° C. This baking makes the screen strong and resistant to chemicals.

The full-size positive is wrapped round the screen now supported on a mandrel. A clear film is tensioned round it to ensure that no light can get underneath, and then the lights are brought down and rotated for the required length of time.

(*Above*) After exposing and developing, the screen is inspected for faults and touched up where necessary.

(*Above, right*) Here, in a close-up of a Johannes Zimmer rotary machine, the screen is being tensioned into correct repeat.

Next the screen must be trimmed down to the correct size – this is about $1\frac{1}{2}$ in. out from the outside repeat crosses. When this is done the end-rings can be fitted. The proper fit of these rings is of the utmost importance for all subsequent work with the screen. Bad fitting may cause breakage to the mesh, and trouble in fitting to the machine. They are of cast alloy and are usually glued with Araldite or a similar adhesive. Each ring has a mark which is carefully set to face the register mark on the screen, so enabling accurate positioning in the printing machine. Finally one end is taped with waterproof tape and numbered to indicate its position in the machine.

Printing with rotary machines

In very simple terms the rotary printing machine consists of the following parts: the cloth feed; a conventional glueing device (and possibly also a thermoplastic glueing device); the screen drive head; a drain; an automatic colour-supply system; a control panel; and the blanket washer. The screens are placed in position (as numbered), the darker colours first. The exact placing is easily determined because, as we have seen, the pitch-mark on the screen has been matched to the mark on the end-ring, and this in its turn is matched to marks on the side of the printing machine.

Some machines, like the Buser, are hydraulically operated, others are electrically run. The cloth is fed into the machine from a big drum and guided over a series of rollers. The belt is furnished with adhesive by roller, and then the belt and the cloth to be printed pass between pressing rollers. As the cloth moves along, it receives the repeat of each colour in turn, the rotary screens being supplied automatically with

colour from the inside. This is pressed through the mesh of the screen by squeegees of varying types. After printing, the cloth is separated from the belt and passes into the drier. The belt passes back underneath the table and into the washing unit. When cleaned and dried, it is then fed back to be gummed again.

The effective brush-type washing device for cleaning the printing blanket is easily accessible at the back of the drive roller. After washing, the blanket is hot-air dried.

SPECIAL FEATURES

To deal with some of the parts of the machine in greater detail, it is interesting to compare the ideas of two or three different firms and see how, although the same basic principle is involved, slightly different solutions have been found.

Different squeegee systems

In the Stork machine, there is a squeegee proper with a squeegee profile and a colour-supply pipe. The special fitting of the holder on to the supply pipe prevents bending of the squeegee even in the case of printing widths of 120 in. or more. Flexible steel strips have proved themselves best; these give even bending and resistance to all chemicals commonly used in printing. The unit is so designed that by adjusting the squeegee vertically, the strip can be bent to the required degree. By lowering the squeegee the strip will be bent more, so increasing the amount of colour printed on to the fabric. The angle of the blade can also be easily adjusted, even during printing, and this adjustment can be read on a scale.

(*Above*) Close-up of a set of rotary screens in operation in a Johannes Zimmer machine.

(*Above, right*) A Zimmer combination machine. The flat screen models can be designed with additional rotary stations. Later on, if the printer wishes, the machine can easily be converted to rotary operation altogether.

Buser machines employ a sophisticated swivel squeegee system which helps to save cloth and colour. This moves up when the printing unit is lifted and is hydraulically moved down when the unit is lowered. Before starting to print, the operator can run colour into one unit after another, because it cannot drip through on to the cloth. After switching on, the printing unit moves down into working position; at the same time the colour runs from the colour basin across the whole width of the screen. This means that right from the first moment of printing the result is clean, not blurred or messy. When printing is finished, or has to be stopped for any reason, the printing unit and swivel squeegee both move up together, the colour in the screen returning to the basin to be pumped back into the colour tank.

Thermoplastic glueing

The Buser machines can be equipped with a thermoplastic glueing device as well as one of the more conventional kind. The thermoplastic adhesive only becomes 'tacky' when heated, and is considered to be more effective. It is a cheaper method, also, as no back-grey is needed, even the sheerest fabrics of synthetic fibre being glued directly to the printing belt. Good printing relies on the cloth being perfectly adhered to the belt and this is why Buser feel that this development is so important. There is a heating unit equipped with

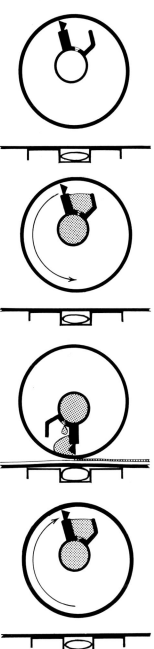

infra-red rods which play on the thermoplastic coated surface and make it tacky. At the same time the cloth passes over the top-side of the unit and is also heated. The rollers, between which the cloth and printing belt pass, press them together and adhesion remains until after printing is complete. Before printing commences the heating unit is in a rest position but when it begins it moves into the working one. Adjustments of heat and roller pressure can be made according to the requirements of various fabrics. Another important point is that as the thermoplastic glue is inactive when cold, ordinary adhesives can be used on top without any detrimental effects.

Peter Zimmer/Kufstein machines

Both the Peter Zimmer/Kufstein and the Johannes Zimmer rotary machines employ the magnet-roll system of pressing the colour through the screen – a process described in the section on flat screen machines, p. 130. There are several other interesting ideas in the Zimmer/Kufstein machines worth noting.

It is probably the wide-width machines from Zimmer/ Kufstein that are the most noteworthy; they have greatly enhanced the market for printed sheets and bedspreads. Wide-width printing – up to 200 in. – has had two or three years' start in the USA and is only now beginning to be more commonly used in England. These extra-wide

The Swiss Buser machines employ a sophisticated swivel squeegee system which helps to save cloth and colour: (1) squeegee arrangement in home position, screen lifted; (2) squeegee arrangement with colour run into colour basin, ready for swinging and lowering for immediate start of printing; (3) printing unit lowered, squeegee in working position, air pad filled; (4) printing unit lifted, squeegee simultaneously swung upward, colour returned from screen to colour basin.

machines can also be used for two-strand printing (the printing of two lengths of fabric at once by putting adhesive tape down the centre of the screen – although this is not always satisfactory).

New developments

Rotary screen printing has proved to be the ideal modern printing method. It has seemingly infinite capacity for adaptability – printing textiles, wallpaper, carpets, vinyl floorcoverings; back and front coating and foam printing; transfer printing; warp printing etc. The most important factor in the industry is flexibility, and it would seem that forecasts made for the method are being widely fulfilled. Not only can rotary screen machines accomplish all of the above but the screens are capable by now of printing most of the fine detail, tonal work and textural effects formerly attributed to engraved rollers as well as much, if not all, which is possible by hand screen. Therefore the method can be used for all classes of work from smaller quantities of sophisticated fabrics to mass production (see p.131: Peter Zimmer's forecast has proven correct). And with the advent of laser engraving of rotary screens in 1986/87, speed (20/30 minutes to engrave a screen), exactness, and an immense variety of styles are possible. Soon all repeat sizes will be possible too (see Chapter 8: Into the Future).

7 Transfer printing

One of the latest and most interesting developments in the field of textile printing of recent years is the process known as transfer, or 'Sublistatic', printing. This is simply a heat-transfer method of patterning synthetic fabrics. The pattern is first printed on to a paper web with special inks usually containing 'dispersed' dyestuffs which sublime at temperatures between 160° and 220° F. (Sublimation is the process in chemistry whereby a solid is converted into a vapour by heat and back again into a solid on cooling.) At this temperature the dyestuffs, which are in their vapour phase, have little affinity for the paper carrier, but a high affinity for the fabric to be printed and thus the image is transferred from the paper to the fabric. The dyestuff is automatically fixed at this temperature and so no further finishing is required.

The majority of polyester, acrylic, acetate and triacetate fibres are suitable for the transfer process, and so is Nylon 6·6. Fabrics woven or knitted from up to 30 per cent natural fibre mixtures also react well to transfer printing, the colours being a little muted but often interestingly subtle. It is a comparatively easy and economic process to print continuous fabric, cut pieces of fully fashioned garments, or even the made-up garments themselves, with a rotary or flat press calendering machine, suitably equipped with a heating unit which can guarantee even heat distribution. On some special presses both top and bottom pieces are heated, allowing both sides of the garment to be printed simultaneously – the time taken varying between fifteen and forty-five seconds, depending on the fibre.

Another point in favour of the method is that bonded fabric can be printed after the bonding has taken place. One serious drawback to the printing of this type of cloth used to be the amount of distortion that resulted, making all but the most nondescript of all-over designs impossible. Now, stripes, checks and exacting geometric patterns are all easily attainable by the transfer process on to the already bonded fabric. Indeed, it is the knitting industry which is beginning to go for transfer printing in a big way, and as knitting is gradually increasing in importance in relation to weaving, it follows that the future of this new method, which was at first thought to be an idea with only a limited appeal, is gaining in its use. It has been estimated that by the end of 1972 the consumption of transfer paper in the UK was running at a rate of 100 million yards a year.

Obviously transfer printing did not mysteriously appear 'out of the blue' without any forerunners or previous experiments. In fact transfer prints on textiles have been produced in various forms – notably as designs to be embroidered – for at least a century. These embroidery transfers, however, were, and are, of a mechanical rather than a chemical variety, using pigment which simply adheres to the cloth.

THE 'STAR' TRANSFER PRINTING PROCESS

In 1953, an Italian process – the 'Star transfer printing process' – was introduced by Stampa Tessuti Artistici of Milan and this was a direct and true forerunner of transfer printing as we know it today. The paper was all photogravure printed and mainly transferred on to natural silk and extremely fine-quality cotton, although also a little on to artificial fibres. The transfer paper was at first in cut sheets, about 36 in. square, say, if the cloth was 36 in. wide, cut on the easiest joining line of the design (but later in continuous rolls), and was passed between pressure rollers at varying temperatures. The big drawback to the Star method was that a normal fixing process was also necessary after transference, and this made it costly and non-competitive.

One of the interesting things about the Star process was that a real attempt was made to exploit some of the exciting effects possible with photogravure and to harness these in repetitive form. This was a difficult task, as gravure printers are finding out now. Most fabric designers are as yet unfamiliar with the endless possibilities of gravure, while graphic artists are in turn lacking in knowledge of repeats and the qualities required in fabric design.

MODERN TRANSFER TECHNIQUES

As early as 1952, ICI took out patents for a sublimation technique which they had evolved, but which subsequently they found was not commercially viable. They did not pursue the process; indeed, they allowed the patents to lapse. In 1960 Noel Déplasse started experimenting and in 1965 Filatures Provoust Masurel, at Roubaix, northern France, finding the patents lapsed, registered the name 'Sublistatic' – a word which has become so completely synonymous with the transfer process as to make one use it (rather embarrasingly at times) when referring to the products of other firms. Noel Déplasse became Director of Société Sublistatic SA and it took about four years before the company reached its full commercial peak. In 1970 Bemrose, an old-established British photogravure printing firm, decided to go into the transfer business with their own patents. The two highly secret aspects of the process, and those which differ slightly from firm to firm, are the composition of the disperse printpaste and the depth of the engraving on the rollers.

Transfer paper can be printed by four different methods: photogravure; flexography; lithography; and screen printing. The first two processes are by far the most widely used; indeed photogravure at first led the field possibly only because the French firm, Provoust Masurel, had the machinery to hand, as had Bemrose of England. However, in the early 1970s flexography made great inroads into the transfer business, and in fact could produce 90 per cent of the designs being used, leaving only 10 per cent which would have to be printed by photogravure by reason of their particular character. (This provided an urgent reason for photogravure firms to begin to exploit more fully the different effects possible by their process.) Lithographic printing from flat plates is only suitable for non-continuous designs; and screen printing also accounts for very little of the market.

There are basically two groups of advantages in the transfer process, those affecting design and those for industry, although these do not necessarily mean that it is in direct competition with roller printing, or flat or rotary screen work; it is simply an additional and useful method.

Design advantages

Because the design is first printed on paper one does not have to rely on the ability of the cloth surface to accept certain effects. With all other methods of printing the cloth structure is of primary importance – a hairy or nobbly surface, loose texture, or other irregularities, are all factors which contribute to loss of definition and which the designer has to consider if a good fabric is to result. Now, for the first time, the design needs only to be something which can be printed on paper, and therefore has very few limitations; the method of putting the design on to the fabric is a quite separate consideration. This gives freedom to the designer, but it also means that he may have to adapt his ideas about fabric design if he is not to be, on the one hand, too conventional in his approach, or on the other, a prey to the temptation of using all sorts of 'gimmicks' for their own sake.

It is possible now to get finely detailed printing from trichromatic photographically separated positives and to produce an infinite number of tonal and colour effects in this way, as well as by all the more usual, well-tried textile techniques. One of the many effects being exploited is one which could be called the 'illusory print', when coarse photographic tweed or knit effects are printed on to much finer and lighter-weight bonded knits. Although these are interesting novelties, it is hoped – and expected – that gradually textile designers will contribute more imaginative photographically based design ideas to the fashion and domestic textile industries.

Also interesting and valuable from the design viewpoint is the fact that exact fitting of colours is achieved at the paper stage, by highly advanced equipment. The photogravure printing machines employ electronic colour registers which control registration to within 0·001 in. This means that some of the best work produced by the transfer method can have the fine detail and precision of colour fit associated with the work seen in many of the old nineteenth-century pattern books.

Industrial advantages

The advantages of transfer printing in industry are numerous, notably in the knitting industry, and are best subdivided into those relating directly to actual fabric production, knitted or otherwise, and those concerned closely with aspects of running the industry generally.

Knitted fabrics, particularly circular ones, nearly always present the printer with a problem, in that the most interesting ones are often rather stretchy and unstable. Great care has to be taken not to extend the cloth before gumming it down and also to gum down securely. It is difficult to get exact colour registration owing to a tendency of the cloth to advance along the print table during printing, so only designs which do not require fine matching are possible on knits by screen or roller printing. With the transfer method all the colours are printed at one operation and so, provided the fabric passes through the rotary calendering machine evenly and without stretching, a sharply defined and accurate print is bound to result. This advantage, of course, applies equally to woven cloth.

As previously mentioned, fabrics that need bonding have this done prior to printing, so making possible all kinds of directional designs which would otherwise be distorted and not remain in line with the straight grain of the cloth.

From the standpoint of running a textile concern there are several points in favour of using the transfer process. First, no special skills are needed to operate either the rotary or the flat calenders used in printing off the cloth. Second, both types of calender are comparatively inexpensive pieces of equipment – from about £7,000 to £10,000. The combination of these two features means that a small printing unit can be set up fairly easily by almost any manufacturer with the resources to do so. Certainly, the idea of having their own printing section is catching on in a number of knitting factories, where in any case they already have calendering machines installed for the heat setting necessary for most synthetic materials; adapted versions of these are all that is required.

Add to these qualities the fact that the transfer method needs no auxiliary printing equipment, such as steamers or washers, and that no stocks of dyes or any other chemicals are necessary. It is also an extremely clean process – because it is a dry technique, floors etc. do not get messy and there is no equipment to wash; and because so little equipment is needed the floor space used is minimal. Water is not used at all in this process; in certain developing countries this is of course a sizeable advantage and one which, in conjunction with the others, may well mean that, in the near future, sales of transfer paper and printing equipment will pull even further ahead than was envisaged.

To the knitted garment industry, the transfer process has the added merit not only of being able to print the back and front of a garment at one and the same time, but being able to heat-set simultaneously as well. Provided the manufacturer, however small, holds sufficient stocks of the transfer paper (which takes up hardly any space), orders can be met in a very short time. It is these qualities of speed and adaptability which are among the most sought after in this competitive era, and stockpiling of unwanted printed cloth can easily be avoided.

PRODUCING A TRANSFER BY PHOTOGRAVURE

The method used for making the gravure rollers varies very little from that described for the production of the photographically engraved machine printing ones (see p. 92). The main differences are that the cylinders are often of silver rather than copper (as in this case silver is the best metal for giving a fine surface), and that the positives are all photographed through extremely fine screens, so producing rollers capable of printing all the subtleties of tone and colour associated with modern photogravure work.

Conventional gravure rollers have all the 'cells', or dots, of the same size but of varying depths, and so can produce all the varying tones from one colour. But recently it has been found that for use in transfer printing the 'hard dot' method is better: the cells are of differing widths but all of the same depth. This type of engraving not only makes a good end-product, but means that the cylinders can be etched automatically. They are rotated in a closed tank of acid for a measured time and brought out etched to a correctly controlled depth. It is important that the etching is not too deep because this would mean that too much colour would be transferred to the cloth, with a possible loss of fastness. If the trichromatic printing technique is to be used, then the design is separated photographically into red, yellow and blue+ black positives, as it would be for normal photogravure work.

Printing the paper

When all the cylinders are completed – six is usually the maximum in any one design – they are fitted in position in the gravure printing machine. This is unlike the textile roller printing machine in that the cylinders are not arranged round a central pressure bowl, but one after the other in a horizontal line. Each colour must be dried before the next is printed as, of course, there is a great deal of close colour work and paper is not so absorbent as cloth. Each roller is supplied with ink (in the case of transfer printing it is still called 'ink' even though it is in fact disperse dyestuff with special additive), has the surplus scraped off by the doctor blade and prints the paper, which then goes up vertically to be dried before coming down again to be printed with the next colour. There is about 20–30 feet of space between each colour printing. Paper up to 80 in. (2,030 mm.) wide can be printed, although the majority of calendering machines at the time of writing are operating at 63 in. (1,600 mm.).

When printed, the colours on the paper do not even remotely resemble the eventual cloth and so it is obvious that, although no special skill is needed to work the machines, the transfer printer must be skilled at matching and sampling. This difficulty is being overcome by the assembling of a growing range of standard shades. After being checked for flaws which, if present, usually occur at the beginnings and ends of the 'web', or roll, the paper is then wound up. It has its edges trimmed and is cut into manageable widths and lengths – rolls 1 yard or more wide, and about 300 yards long, and weighing 28–36 lb.

Another interesting feature worth mentioning is that single-colour cloths can be produced from paper printed by means of a specially engraved cylinder. This paper gives to the cloth a solid-shade dyeing effect. The correct matching of printed and plain cloths can thus easily be arrived at. Anyone who has experienced the difficulties of getting a piece-dyed shade to match a printed fabric will readily appreciate the significance of this.

When the printed cloth is needed, all the manufacturer has to do is to place the printed transfer in contact with the particular cloth in the calendering machine (either rotary or flat), apply the correct heat necessary for the fibre, along with the right pressure, and in fifteen to thirty seconds the dye on the paper is vaporized and the cloth is patterned and ready, on cooling, for use without any further processing. The flat-bed calendering machines can print easily across the seams of made-up jumpers and dresses, though they are usually of course only semi-continuous in operation. But the rotary types used in the production of yardage have continuous outputs of up to 15 yards a minute. The type of rotary machine supplied by Hunt and Moscrop Limited, among others, uses a heated cylinder and an endless blanket. Once pressure is applied, contact time is only about half a minute. Other types use a vacuum to hold the paper and cloth in contact, and heat is supplied by infra-red units; these machines are claimed to be good because, as there is no mechanical pressure, there is no way for the fabric or garment to get damaged. It is, however, a much slower method, completing about only 2 or 3 yards a minute.

Disadvantages

There are some limitations to the transfer method, of course, one of these being that at present it is only really successful on polyester, polyamide and acrylic fibres or blends, and on acetate and triacetate fibres. But owing to high temperatures needed for sublimation, it is not possible on low-melting-point fibres, for instance certain nylons, polypropylene and PVC fibres. There has been some criticism of the fastness properties on Nylon 6·6 and triacetates and it is often felt that they are better if steamed afterwards. However, one firm has also perfected transfer printing on wool using acid dyes. Here a steam or electrically heated press is used at temperatures of about 110° C.

The transfer paper is fairly costly and yardage printing does not become economic until after 10,000 yards. One criticism often levelled is that at a time when textile factories are cutting down and streamlining their organizations, the transfer method introduces another complete process; but the ease and economy with which the rest of the printing is done must surely go a long way towards counterbalancing this. And while the addition of the paper stage may be considered an unnecessary one by many older textile manufacturers it does at least bring with it the solid advantage that any faults can be seen and corrected at this cheaper stage rather than on the much more expensive cloth.

A number of firms ran a commission printing service for the paper, as well as developing their own collections for sale. Among these were Bemrose, English Calico's Transprints UK Ltd, and ICI's Inprint collection, Société Sublistatic SA of France also established a subsidiary in Great Britain. In the USA in November 1972, the first transfer printing plant was set up by ITP America in Commack, Long Island.

Postscript

Transfer printing as a method has certainly not lived up to expectations and many companies became bankrupt. This was, of course, partly due to the disenchantment with double-knit polyester and the move back to rayon and cotton. Experiments in transferring onto these fibres continue.

FLEXOGRAPHIC PRINTING

The idea of cutting relief images in rubber has been used for many years for the printing of corrugated paper and packing-cases, but it is only in the last ten years or so that it has begun to be used in cylinder form for Duplex printing of furnishing fabrics. And then, in 1969, Cobden Chadwick Limited of Oldham produced a machine for wallpaper work, and in 1970 for transfer printing. In the latter field it shares almost

Direct cutting of the flexographic
roller.

equal popularity with photogravure work. It was the advent
of polythene in the packaging industry that first aroused
interest in this type of machine.

Considering the surprising fineness of line and detail
possible in the reliefs, it is amazing that the material has not
been exploited more fully previously. Probably the two
main reasons for the sudden increase in the use and development of the method are the advances both in rubber technology, and in moulding techniques; these last have made
great strides as a result of work in plastics. But aside from
these reasons, transfer printing itself is becoming so much
more popular than was anticipated, particularly in Great
Britain (proportionately more than in other countries), that
it has provided a big outlet and incentive for development.

Making flexographic cylinders

The cylinders for direct fabric printing, for use in Duplex
work, are always made of neoprene – a synthetic rubber –
because this is resistant to white spirit, urea, water and other
substances used in printpastes. But the ones made for
transfer printing consist of natural rubber.

For whichever industry they are intended, the patterned
cylinders are made in one of two ways. The pattern can be
cut directly into the surface of the rubber roller – a method
used for the less detailed designs. Alternatively, several
rubber stereos are made and fixed with adhesive, in repeat

A close-up to show the way the ground is cleared.

positions, on to the surface of a rubber cylinder (this method is used for finer and more intricate work). Some designs need a combination of the two types of cylinder.

It is worth mentioning that, because of the close and accurate fitting of colours required for the transfer printing paper, hand painting of positives is not much used. Instead a master stencil is made by lining in all the colour areas with a special cutter on a gelatine-coated stencil. This is then used to produce a master positive. From this positive all the colour separations are made (again on coated stencils), by cutting and lifting off the pattern areas from the protective backing. For the first method of roller making, a full-size positive is of course needed, but for the second it is necessary only to produce an area of repeat the same size as the stereo required.

When making a cylinder by direct cutting, the full-size positive is first wrapped round the rubber cylinder, which has been coated with photographic emulsion, and the pattern is photographed on to this cylinder. The cylinder is then placed on a mandrel and the cutter 'skives', or pares away, the outer limits of the shapes to be cut away, and then removes the background to a depth considered sufficient for the use to which the particular roller will be put. It is important that the walls of the relief shapes should be cut sloping out at an angle instead of vertically, to ensure sufficient support at the base. Because it is very easy for a positive to twist out of position slightly when it is wound round the

The zinc plate from which the Bakelite mould is made.

cylinder, subsequent colour rollers have their patterns printed on to them, each in turn, from the previously cut roller. This ensures that, if there is a slight fault, each cylinder will still match up with the others in the set.

To make a cylinder built up from a series of rubber stereos, each colour separation is photographed on to a zinc plate and subsequently acid-etched. Alternatively it can be photographed on to a 'Dycril'-polypropylene plate and etched with caustic soda. From this etched plate a Bakelite mould is made. Bakelite powder is dusted over the mould before placing it in the press, to maximize the depth of the finished stereo. A piece of unvulcanized rubber of the correct size is then placed in the press in contact with the mould and the heat and pressure vulcanize and form the rubber. It has then to be cured for about seven minutes. All the stereos are then placed into correct repeat positions round the circumference of a rubber roller and fixed with a strong adhesive. In the early days of making flexographic rollers the positioning had to be laboriously carried out by careful measuring, but now sophisticated 'Opticheck' machines are available which can be set to the correct repeat sizes and make the job completely accurate as well as speedy. The rollers must then be placed on a mandrel and more deeply cut in places, by hand. When the design is finished with, the rubber can be 'turned off' and the roller re-used.

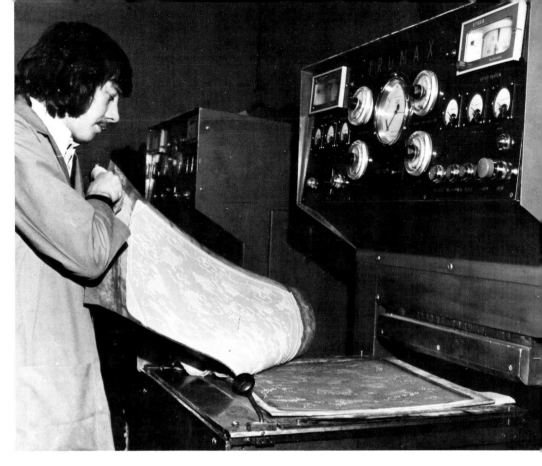

The formed and vulcanized rubber stereo being removed from the press.

The completed roller formed from a number of stereos; the joins can be seen in the photograph, but the print from the rollers is absolutely even all over.

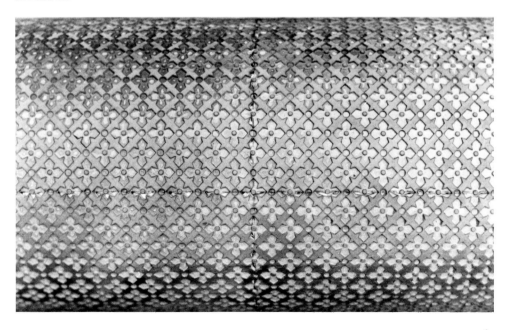

The printing process

As far as transfer printing is concerned, most of the flexo-graphic printing machines are suitable for six colours, and are of the single-impression cylinder type (having a single central pressure bowl). This central pressure bowl, or impression cylinder, is of steel – weighing several tons – and is so finely surfaced and measured as to be exact in diameter to less than a thousandth of an inch. A rubber roller rotates in the colour trough and then transfers its colour to an 'anilox' cylinder which in turn supplies a controlled amount of colour to the pattern roller. The 'anilox' roller has a steel core lined with copper. This is engraved with about 165 cells to the square inch, and finally chromed (as in engraved roller printing), to extend its life. Different scales are used, but 165 is considered good for a wide variety of work.

When the machine runs at about 200 feet per minute, it is unnecessary to air-dry between colours – merely to have tunnel-drying after the printing is completed is enough. But if the machine is to be run at 300–350 feet per minute it is essential to have a warm air drier unit installed between each colour station (or nip). The amount of colour applied can be varied simply by altering the speed of the rubber inking roller. An important point to note in flexographic transfer printing, as indeed in photogravure, is the quality of paper needed. If it is too absorbent it will obviously not give up sufficient dyestuff on subliming, whereas if the surface is too hard it will cause a 'pressing out' of colour, leading to subsequent 'shadowing' in the print on cloth.

Flexography has a part to play in Duplex direct fabric printing as well as transfer work. Flexographic cylinders are used in the English Calico 'Stalwart' machine, patented in the late 1950s by John Bolton and his colleagues. This machine was constructed by the Stalwart Engineering Company to their design, and was later sold to the CPA (Calico Printers' Association, now English Calico*). Only three machines were built. The printing cylinders are arranged in a vertical form, so the running of the machine is simple. Although very accurate registration of colours is impossible with this arrangement, it is considerably better than the ordinary Duplex, and has the advantage that when pigments are used the amount of colour deposited on the cloth is less than from the Aljaba machine; this means that the resulting cloth is much less stiff.

Flexography was slow to take off in the US but now computerized laser cutting is being used for the production of the cylinders.

* Known as Tootal Ltd since July 1973.

8 Into the future

Since 'Manual of Textile Printing' was first published, immense changes and developments have taken place in the field of textile printing. These changes are almost all related to computerization – in design (C.A.D.); film making and screen engraving (with electronically controlled lasers); and automated print machines, all functions of which can be monitored and controlled from a computer terminal.

The speed, accuracy and flexibility which can result from these automated systems are highly desirable qualities, particularly at this time – and in the foreseeable future. 'Quick response' – the phrase used to indicate a system which allows the producer to respond immediately to the demands of the consumer or client, has become the watchword.

The Sci-Tex system

In 1975 the Sci-Tex response system 200 was first used commercially at Tootal Ltd (Manchester). Developed entirely for the textile industry, (unlike many that came later which were adapted), it could perform many of the tasks that computerized equipment performs today, even though at slower speeds and with less memory.

This first Sci-Tex could scan original designs or contour areas for colour separation. Repeats could be closed; step and repeat work performed; designs mirrored, etc. With the use of a digital pen, subtle changes could be made in shape, texture and line, to the image viewed on the monitor. Very importantly also, Sci-Tex could generate the 'allowance' (or 'trap') required for those colour areas of the pattern which were in contact with each other. The Sci-Tex could screen for galvano and other engraving productions. Finally, full-size films could be produced from the digital information by interfacing with a laser exposing machine.

Since the early 1980s many systems, mostly P.C. based, have been developed and Sci-Tex itself has changed and improved. But it is worth noting that for a long time it was unique in the textile industry.

C.A.D. systems are used in great numbers in converters' studios, where the digitized designs can be re-coloured, re-worked and repeated many times swiftly (instead of the average 2–17 times re-drawing by hand). Also designs can be reduced or enlarged and reorganized for a variety of coordinating products.

In the engraver's studio much time is saved by sending designs, already separated, to generate film (i.e. the computer file is sent).

Colour separations

Original designs can be scanned to generate colour separations, but although there are improvements in this area, usually some 'cleaning up' is required. The main source of trouble is that often the original design has been painted in close-tone colours – even when these are opaque. If, however, they are in 'water-colour' or charcoal effects (the type of designs most difficult to separate manually anyway), problems are much greater. In the United States, where speed and automation are considered more important than experience, designers working for large companies are sometimes asked to paint their designs in very clearly defined colours, in order to facilitate electronic separation techniques – presumably thus presenting a design of a totally different character!

Before discussing further developments in screen engraving, it is interesting to note points with regard to some problems – the biggest of which is that of 'resolution' (i.e. 'd.p.i.' or 'dots per inch').

*1   As a designer, if you just want to lay out a design and experiment with colours and ideas, you can do this on a P.C. (Mactintosh etc.) with 72 d.p.i. But you would need to repaint the design on paper before you could sell it.

2   To design on the computer and print out professionally enough to sell, 300/400 d.p.i. would be needed.

3   Digitized information for engraving, however, needs to employ at least 500/1,000 d.p.i. In order to satisfy the condition of the screens (i.e. 185 mesh up to 265), at least twice as much data would be needed – around 500, but up to 1,000 d.p.i. for the best results.

High resolution needs bigger computer storage – even a small design of 12 inch square repeat with 8 colours needs a whole disk. There is also a speed problem.

No systems exist at present which can take a design through to engraving. Transfers have to be made (so it is very important that systems can interface with each other). The development of one that can do the whole job is the work of the 1990s.

Laser engraving

In 1986 textile technology journals gave the first intimations of the viability of a new process for engraving rotary screens. In 1987, the equipment developed by Schablonentechnik of Austria was commercially produced and marketed by Stork of Holland as the STK 2000 laser engraver for the first time.

Earlier attempts to engrave nickel screens had proved to be

*Analysis from Mary Howard, Athena Design Systems, Inc., Boston.

too costly and were therefore abandoned. Finally, a very simple solution was found. The perforated screen was given a protective coating and then the laser used to burn away this coating, making for an economic use of energy and a successful laser engraver.

Since 1987 the number of laser engraving machines in the United States and Europe has grown rapidly and praise for them is universal.

1 It is possible to engrave a standard 640mm ($25\frac{1}{4}''$) screen in 20/30 minutes (instead of up to 185 minutes previously), depending on style of design.
2 Extreme accuracy is easily achieved – the circumference of the base screen is divided digitally into repeats, therefore, any slight variation in circumference size between screens is no longer a problem.
3 There is no joining of film as engraving is by rotary motion.
4 Full-size film is not needed. Small films are still used, but soon, particularly as it becomes more difficult to find qualified design tracers, original designs will all be scanned, revised, manipulated and engraved without using film.
5 Half-tone work is becoming much easier and it is desirable to use laser engraving for this purpose (instead of the galvano technique which has pollution problems). A good half-tone screen can replace three or four solid colour screens and get the same effect – so it is an economical and effective method of design.

There are two companies manufacturing laser equipment: Stork (Boxmeer, Holland) with the STK 2000 and ZET Instruments Ltd (England), with the Zedco Screen laser engraving system.

By 1990 Stork had installed about 30 systems in the United States and many elsewhere, and although all screen meshes are usable, the most common in use are 125 for apparel and 105 for domestic textiles. There is so much work for the technique that little time has been given to experimenting with half-tone work (in the United States) which is still produced mainly by galvano.

'New computer technology allows direct colour scanning; higher resolution; unlimited repeat sizes (in widths up to 46 inches); and makes all the steps up to the actual engraving simple and quick, therefore needing less training time.'*

In 1991 Stork introduced new screen types involving a new plating technique in sizes 135; 165 and 195 mesh.

A great advantage, certainly in America, where high volume usage and/or damage often requires screens to be quickly remade in the middle of a print run, is the exactness of reproducibility. For this reason, a number of printers have installed a laser engraver, so that they (not their screen maker), can re-engrave the necessary screen from the digital information supplied. It has also been found that as a result of the exactness, print machines can be set up more quickly with

*Copeland Willis of Stork Screens (America)

little or no adjustment of screen settings.

ZED Instruments Ltd (England) has for years produced machinery for the laser engraving of flexographic and others, and several years ago developed their Zedco laser engraving machine for rotary screens. The Zedco is a highly regarded piece of equipment which also has many very important features including very fast loading and unloading; swift change of repeat size; an auto calibration option which measures the open areas of a screen dynamically – 'this means that we can remake an old half-tone job on a new screen with a different lacquer type or thickness and exactly reproduce a copy engraving'.* Half-tones can be engraved directly from digital data or scanned washes and charcoals – this ability seems to be one of the particularly important features of the machine.

*Keith Davies of Zedco

Control of print machines

Before leaving rotary screen printing and engraving, the computer regulation of the actual print machine must be mentioned. This includes:
- automatic speed control of blanket and screen drive
- automatic repeat setting
- automatic height adjustment of screens
- adjustment of pressure and angle of squeegee or magnet-roll systems

All these types of settings can be manually adjusted and then put into the memory of the control system. All the major producers of rotary screen printing machines have similar process controls.

Inkjet printing technologies

The first ink-jet system for the patterning of textiles was the 'Millitron', developed by Milliken and Company (United States) in 1974/75 which has printed millions of yards of carpet, pile upholstery fabric and rugs.

This is based on 'dot matrix' technologies in which 'minute drops of ink, squirted from a nozzle and steered in flight can be made to form printed characters' – and is obviously well suited to printing at the command of a computer – i.e. directly from a computer aided design (C.A.D.) system memory; scanned patterns; pictures or photographs and with, therefore, potentially no design limitations.

There are several different methods of 'drop steering' by electric charges, or the use of magnetic ink controlled by magnetic fields, for instance.

In the Millitron, the dye liquor is kept in circulation by a pump and individual electro-magnetic valves control jets of air blowing onto the continuous 'curtain of dye liquor'. When required for the pattern, the valves seal off the air and

the jets drop colour onto the carpet, otherwise the dye is recycled. 10–16 jets per inch are used to pattern carpets and pile upholstery fabric.

The Zedco Screen laser engraving system produces rotary screens at high speed without sacrificing quality.

There are many advantages to the ink-jet system, the most obvious being the unlimited pattern size; flexibility and ease of change from one pattern to the next. It is a quiet process; only wasting about two inches of fabric at the changeover and can be economical for sampling and short runs.

The Millitron is also controlled by a Sci-Tex pattern control system. New ideas have resulted from this, for example, adapting the method to the production of fabric using filament deflection.

The jet control method used in the Millitron is one that cannot be adapted to produce much higher resolution. For fine resolution (i.e. about 100–300 d.p.i.), a system of D.O.D. (drop-on-demand) or continuous flow with electrostatic control is required.

It is also easy to see that dye stuff composition and filtration is extremely important. The dye has to penetrate the fabric (unlike paper) and the width of textile fabrics and speed of operation are important considerations. Lou Graham, a leading researcher and expert in the field, formerly with Burlington Research Laboratories, estimates that for current textile widths and speeds, the electronic data rate for transfer of detailed design information would be about one billion decisions per second!

Among experiments in several countries, the European Economic Community established Eureka, an advanced research facility. A grant was given to a consortium of Stork X-cel BV (Holland); Proll of Germany, and a Swedish university for research into ink jet printing for various products.

In fact in 1990 Stork marketed an ink-jet printer for the sampling of designs on cloth – a useful addition to sampling equipment allowing customers to view the pattern on cloth prior to screens being made.

The Stork X-cel ink-jet printer with its 'prediction proofer' which enables designs to be sampled prior to the screens being made.

Colour measurement and matching

Since the late 1960s and early 1970s, A.C.S. (Applied Color Systems, Inc., now ACS Datacolor) of Princeton, United States; I.C.S. (Instrumental Colour Systems) England, and others, have developed systems linking instrumental colour measurement to many functions vital to the running of most print labs and print plants.

The original colour of a design can have its reflectance measured by a spectrophotometer and the information compared with data stored in a shade library. Data can include recipe prediction; storage and calculations; stock control; details of metamerism; cost factors; availability etc. Most print plants these days are equipped with a computerized colour measurement system and many have some form of automatic or semi-automatic paste dispensing system.

Automatic paste dispensing

The first automatic paste dispensing system on the market was the Texicon (United Kingdom) in the early 1970s. A number of early difficulties were encountered but these were finally ironed out. The Texicon Autoweigh 2 and 3, are widely used as are the Stork IPS 2000 (Holland); the Van Wyk

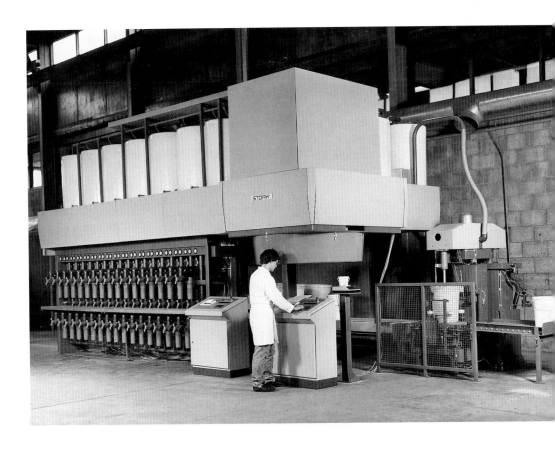

The Stork I.P.S. 2000 automatic paste dispensing system.

System (Holland) and the C.I.R. (Italy). All, except C.I.R., are gravimetric systems – i.e. each component of the print paste is weighed automatically. The volumetric system does need continual recalibration and the valves are subject to wear, particularly so when used for abrasive pigment and vat systems.

From the relevant data stored in the computer, these systems can be used to dispense automatically all the ingredients in the recipe selected, and in quantities ranging from those needed for lab samples e.g. 300gms, to production quantities of between 120kg and 1000kg. It is extremely important to make sure that the system will dispense the range of quantities required by the print plant.

Perhaps the most important feature of the equipment is its valves, which have separate flow rates to dispense in jet gradations from full, through medium, fine and 'stuttering' (the Stork term for final droplet dispensing).

The Stork IPS 2000 has a specially designed mixer and tub scraper which cleans the sides of the tub and directs the mass to the middle ensuring complete integration. Computerized control of the 'colour kitchen' ensures that there will be correlation between production and sampling and, for companies with small yardage production of many multicoloured designs, a good system can mix as many as 2,500 sample and production buckets of paste per week.

This brief outline of the great changes that have taken place since the mid-1970s and which will continue rapidly in the future can be summed up very concisely in the following way:*

*Ciba-Geigy Basel

Success factors for future oriented mills

— readiness to adopt modern technologies fitting in with the company specific situation
— open partnership during the implementation of hi-tech systems
— ready to meet stringent quality requirements
— positive approach to the solution of environmental problems
— provision of working stations with a high standard of hygiene

Future requirements

— fast adoption of international fashion trends
— speedy and flexible handling of orders
— utilization of chances arising from eco-political changes (new economic areas, new countries emerging as industrial powers, exchange rate fluctuations)

9 Design and industry

To turn to the subject of design, it is interesting to see how basically unchanging are the attitudes of designers and industrialists over the years. There was in the early nineteenth century, as indeed there always has been, a great deal of talk about mechanization lowering standards. And there is no doubt that the machine age did usher in the production of vast quantities of badly designed goods; but as far as printed textiles are concerned, when one looks back at the intricately engraved patterns of the 1830 to 1880 period, it is hard to believe that it was the strong criticism of English prints and scathing comparisons with French designs that brought about the establishment of schools of design in England.

One of the earlier objections to machine printing seems to indicate mere snobbery, as in the remark: 'What person would willingly give five or six shillings a yard if their servants can have an imitation or what has nearly the effect for two or three?'; or the tart observation that 'a country wake of the nineteenth century may display as much finery as a drawing-room of the eighteenth century'.

Of course, the designs that were machine printed had, of necessity, to be different in character from hand printed ones; for instance the vertical repeat was at first between 9 and 12 inches – and this, while being reasonable for dress fabrics, greatly curtailed the inventiveness of furnishings. But when new production methods are introduced the pitfall is always to try to use old design ideas instead of rethinking the problem and so getting the most interesting solution. The best results do not come until an acceptance and an understanding of the new methods enables the designer to use them to his advantage in creating new ideas.

But undoubtedly, the design of English printed cottons was considered by many to be vastly inferior to the European designs, particularly the French ones. Even in 1791, Charles O'Brien in his *British Manufacturers Companion* was very positive about the reasons for the French supremacy and the way in which English fabrics could be improved. From the very earliest days of printing at Jouy, in France, Oberkamphe's emphasis was on quality in every way; he advocated designs commissioned from talented artists and designers, first-rate craftsmen, fast colours, and strong encouragement for new ideas and methods (but only after sufficient experiment). His long and varied experience (he was apprenticed at eleven years old) in dyeing and printing, designing and engraving made him an outstanding owner-manager for a printworks. His natural appreciation of design and colour as well as his technical skill made him able to get the best out of designers and printers, and although he died in 1815, when machine printing was only just beginning to be used, the tradition of a high standard in fabric design and printing was firmly established in France and has continued to the present day.

But in England, possibly because so many of the inventions in the cotton industry were British in origin, the full force of mechanization swept through the textile industry with such speed that the country was very quickly committed to almost total mass production. Hand spinning and weaving, and also block printing, were continued in the country areas as cottage industries well into the twentieth century; but in the towns the number of mass-production factories rose swiftly. A journalist in the early nineteenth century commented:

> ... the cylinder machine, attended by one man to regulate the rollers, is capable of printing as many pieces as a hundred men and a hundred girls could with the hand-block during the same time; or as much work may be executed by a cylinder machine in 4 minutes as by the ordinary method of block printing in six hours. A length of calico equal to one mile has been printed off with 4 different colours in a single hour.

By 1850 many more engraved roller printing machines were in use; at the Broadoak Printworks (later part of the CPA) 300 fewer people were employed as a result of the gradual extension of cylinder printing and the decline of hand block printing. But the output everywhere continued to increase as the home and export markets demanded more and more yardage. In the mid-eighteenth century only about 50,000 pieces of mixed cloth were printed in the whole of Great Britain, whereas by 1850 several manufacturers turned out as much as 300,000 to 400,000 pieces *each* per annum.

Frederick Engels, the German nineteenth-century social historian, said: 'the new arrangements in the printworks have superseded the hand-workers much more than was the case in the production of the fabrics'. A petition by the printers presented in the House of Commons in the year 1842 stated that out of the 11 million pieces of printed cotton goods only 100,000 were printed exclusively by hand, 900,000 partly with machinery and 10 million by machinery alone with four to six colours. With the new machinery constantly being improved, eventually only about a quarter of the hand printers could be fully employed, the rest either being totally without work or employed for one, two or three days per week.

France did not take quite so quickly to cylinder printing and by 1850 far fewer were in use there. So right at the beginning of the industrial era there was this parting of the ways – English firms chose to emphasize the mass-production side in order to supply the ever-increasing Empire market, while the French were more concerned with using all new developments to further the production of fabrics with an emphasis on good design as well as on profit making. And even as early as the first years of the nineteenth century, not only were the wealthy in England buying French printed fabrics, but English printers were buying French designs, and have gone on doing so ever since.

The Society for the Encouragement of Arts, Manufactures and Commerce (now known as the Royal Society of Arts), had been founded in England in 1754 to encourage public art education and to further the interest in the design of everyday products. Competitions were started as early as 1758 for printed and woven fabrics, among other things. But in spite of this, between 1810 and 1835 the situation with regard to English design was considered to be so bad that the government set up a 'Select Committee on Arts and their Connection with Manufactures'. Many manufacturers who gave evidence before the committee were unanimous in their condemnation of the work of English designers and admitted that they used only French designs – even those kept for several decades being considered better and more fashionable than English ones.

The outcome of the report was the setting up of schools of design in 1836; the main one was in London, with others in the provinces, of which the first to be given official recognition was Manchester, in 1842. Within a few years others were set up in London, Sheffield, the Potteries, Coventry, Nottingham, Huddersfield and elsewhere. One of the important results expected from these schools was that they would train people to be able to compete with the French and Germans in the field of cotton print designing and so encourage English manufacturers to cut down on the purchasing of European ideas. But, mainly owing to unsatisfactory conditions caused by a series of arguments about the relevance of a fine-art training for intending designers and the absence of practical instruction, it was found that industrialists continued to buy from abroad. In 1847 forty firms were circularized to find out to what extent they used designers trained in the schools. It was found that fewer than one-fifth of the people involved in pattern designing had attended the schools, and also that French designs were still being bought as much as ever.

In 1849 the students at the Central School of Design in London decided among themselves that if they wanted to be accepted as designers for calico printing or anything else, they needed above all some instruction in the practical aspects of industry. In a lecture delivered to the class by a fellow student the following comments were made:

The greatest obstacle is, doubtless, the very general ignorance of the students as to the manufacturing processes to which their designs must, in more or less every case, be adapted. This circumstance renders the designs produced in the school so usually unfitted for manufacture, as to make them practically useless. It matters little enough that a design possesses every artistic excellence, if it be incapable of adaption to a manufactured article; and while our manufacturers, by importing French patterns (in Manchester alone to the amount of above £20,000 per annum), can obtain exactly what is suited to their purpose, it is not to be expected they will purchase what is not.

The students felt that a great deal of the trouble could be remedied by well-illustrated lectures by competent people.

True as all this was, some of the fault undoubtedly lay with the manufacturers, for being unwilling to try different ideas, and for not being prepared to experiment with the methods at their disposal to help in the realization of these ideas. It always has been slightly paradoxical that the industrialist whose keenest interest is in design, colour and style will get the best out of any method of production, and will often succeed in developing new techniques and, certainly, in refining older ones. In his efforts to create on cloth the best rendering of the newer and more varied designs the enlightened and creative textile producer will employ the most experienced technicians and be on the alert for any practical ideas or developments which contribute to this end. On the other hand, the manufacturer who is interested in mechanical inventions for the sole purpose of speed and increased profit will often short-sightedly reject ideas because he has not the imagination to see their ultimate value, or as O'Brien states, he will be 'more alive to immediate "Loss and Gain" than to distant advantage' – he often refuses to give credence to new ideas which would not only advance printing techniques and produce better cloths, but ultimately make for greater profits.

Many people felt strongly that English designers were as good as the French and that preference for their work was supported rather by fashion than by judgment, but that the lack of protection made the cost-conscious manufacturer loth to pay out any apparently needless money if his designs were going to be copied in a few months. In 1842 an Act of Parliament granted copyrights for designs in different fields. These varied from three to twelve months, and even up to three years, but in 1850 the Act was changed to make the copyright period four years for all designs.

THE NEW DYES

Comparable changes took place in the nineteenth century in the field of dye chemistry. Until the 1850s all dyestuffs were natural in origin. The 'vegetable' colours, for instance indigo, madder and saffron, were then added to by the 'mineral' colours such as antimony orange, Prussian blue and manganese brown, which had been introduced in the late eighteenth century. It was at this time, particularly in France, that a dye chemistry based on scientific principles began to grow up.

Almost all dyes had to be used in conjunction with 'drugs' or mordants which in the nineteenth century were basically defined as of two types. The 'mordants proper' were metallic salts such as alum, tin, iron and copper, whose oxides effect a chemical union with the fibre and colouring matter. The second group, known as 'not true mordants', were those which, while having an affinity for the colouring matter, do not combine with the cloth fibres chemically, but which rather adhere to them mechanically. This class consists of oils, albumen, casein, etc. As we have seen in Chapter 1 on Indian palampores, the metallic oxides used in different strengths produce from madder a range of colours: black, brown, crimson, pinks, lilacs, purple. As for the second group, the vegetable and animal mordants adhere either by exposure to air (as the oil in Turkey-red dyeing), or they are fixed by heat, as is the albumen in pigment colours.

The early years of the nineteenth century saw a great deal of research into the application of dyestuffs and experiments with the use of different chemicals to facilitate this. The science became highly developed, particularly in France, and later also in Germany and England. It is recorded that in England a prize of £2,000 was offered for a 'solid green' dye which was unobtainable anywhere in the world. (Green had always been produced by printing or 'pencilling' a dull yellow over blue which gave a dull, weak green, and the yellow part, at least, was very fugitive, even in Indian textiles.) The prize was thought to have been won in Britain, but the results were so unconvincing that the credit was later (in 1809) accorded to a Frenchman, Samuel Widmer, relative and colleague of Oberkamphe; he revealed his discovery in return for being shown an English three-colour engraved cylinder machine.

As well as the development of mineral colours, other discoveries were made, such as the production of 'Garancin' in 1828. It was found that a very concentrated madder dye could be made by steeping the roots of the madder plant in sulphuric acid. The acid acted on the woody fibres, setting far more of the colouring matter free, accounting for the strong, saturated deep crimsons, browns and burnt oranges of the Garancin style.

The high point of the experiments was the development of aniline dyes from coal-tar – the first being known as Perkin's Purple, discovered in 1856 by a Manchester chemist, W.H. Perkin, when he was only nineteen years old. In 1859 magenta, named after the French victory at Magenta in north Italy, was discovered, and finally in 1869 alizarin, the

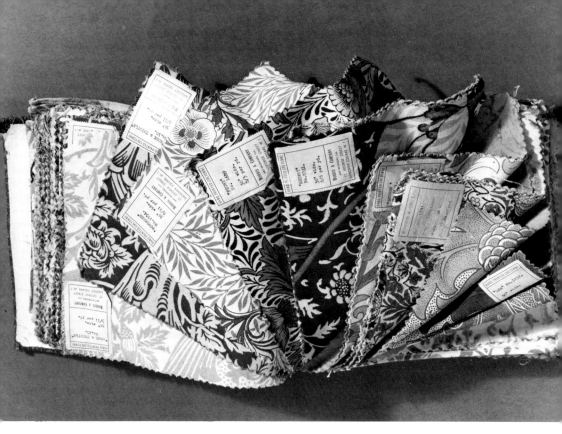

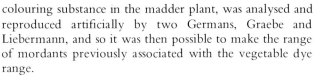

(*Above*) A pattern book from Morris & Co., Hanover Square. The date is unknown, but is probably about the turn of the century. (*Below*) Morris's design for the *Daffodil* chintz.

colouring substance in the madder plant, was analysed and reproduced artificially by two Germans, Graebe and Liebermann, and so it was then possible to make the range of mordants previously associated with the vegetable dye range.

WILLIAM MORRIS AND DESIGN

It was the sharpness and crudeness of the first new colours, as well as the poor quality of the designs, that caught the notice of William Morris and his friends and resulted in the founding, in 1861, of Morris, Marshall, Faulkner and Company. It is of course for the design of his chintz (as well as wallpapers) that Morris is best known today, although the production of these fabrics occupied a short period of his working life, the great majority being printed between 1875 and 1885.

Morris found that already in the comparatively few years since mechanization many of the old crafts had died out – or very nearly so. It is surprising that in 1874, when Morris wanted to find out at first hand about the old vegetable dyeing methods he could find only Thomas Wardle of Leek, a dyer who remembered a great deal from his boyhood, to help him. Morris was able to refer to old books and herbals, but it is nevertheless astonishing that within so few years of the development of artificial dyes the old methods should have been discarded. In *Dyeing and Calico Printing*, published in 1874, W. Crookes gave very detailed accounts of the use of madder and indigo methods, but apparently these were not much used by the late 1870s.

Morris's chintz were all blockprinted by coppered blocks, and after various experiments he used the old indigo dyeing techniques and discharged with soda or potash, sometimes reprinting the colours in the discharged areas afterwards. He used a wood block for the 'bleach' or discharge. But although he went back to the Gothic period for much of his design and to the early days of calico printing for dye techniques and block printing, he did not entirely reject modern methods or even the factory system. Most of his chintz, his wallpapers and woven cloths were produced in other people's factories, and later, in 1880, he set up his own print-works at Merton Abbey. But he organized this according to his own beliefs, arranging shorter working hours than the Factory Acts laid down, paying higher wages than the normal, and instituting a partial profit-sharing system. He planted trees and flowers round the printworks (which was a disused older one near the river Wandle) and tried in every way to make it an agreeable place to work.

Although he was not an original thinker, gaining most of his ideas from people like Ruskin, Rossetti, Carlyle, Marx and many others, he was one of the few who tried in every way to carry out all his ideas and those he admired in others.

A William Morris 'bleach' or discharge block made of wood and felt: the *Evenlode* chintz, 1883.

Block printing at the Morris works, Merton Abbey.

His belief that everything people make or use should be as well designed as possible, and his dream that 'every man's home will be fair and decent and that every man will have his share of the best', he did all in his power to carry out, even to the extent of pouring out most of his money in support of these ideals.

Today, with our increased interest in the environment and concern for the better quality of life, we can readily accept many of his ideas; but it is still as a designer that he has had the biggest influence in England and elsewhere. Yet in the nineteenth century the Arts and Crafts Movement, in which he played a leading part, made a far greater impact on European textile producers than on manufacturers in England. In the ten years from 1874, because his private fortune had almost gone and he needed to make some money from the firm, he designed and produced eleven wallpapers and twenty-two chintz. Few would dispute that he was the greatest single designer of decorative patterns ever, and in quantity as well as quality: he designed over five hundred patterns for various mediums.

But although his hatred of modern machinery was very strong – unlike C.F. Voysey, another keen member of the Arts and Crafts Movement, who regarded the machine not as an enemy but as something to use to the best advantage – Morris still had the vision to foresee the ultimate benefits that it could bring in the way of increased leisure:

> We should be masters of our machines and not their slaves ... it is not this or that tangible steel or brass machine which we want to get rid of, but the great intangible machine of commercial tyranny.

Paul Thompson in his book on Morris, in which he comments on the great gulf between Morris's ideas and his work as a designer and manufacturer, wrote:

> His ideas, his belief that men's work should be creative and satisfying, that design should be based on respect for material and technique, are still immediate today ... but they [his designs] were mostly made in small quantities for wealthy clients and they were nearly always produced by monotonous work processes, whether by factory artisans or by bored Victorian ladies.

And it is for the quality of his designs that Morris will always be significant, while his aim that every man should be able to afford (and should desire) well-designed fabrics, or anything else for his home, is likely to be achieved only through education and the enlightened use of the mass-production methods he so disliked.

William Morris *Eye Bright* chintz, 1883. This is one of Morris's fabrics using a dyed indigo ground with a full and a half discharge, giving a pattern in deep blue, light blue and white.

Glossary

Fixation of printed colour by means of heat or steam. AGEING
Originally induced by the action of air, sunlight and dew, this process gradually came to be carried out in large ageing rooms, and now in a 'rapid ager' (or hot-air or steam cabinet).

The essential colouring matter of the madder root, now ALIZARIN
produced artificially from anthracene, a coal-tar derivative.

In engraved roller printing, a small space between areas of ALLOWANCE
colour, so carefully calculated as to be just closed on printing – to avoid bleeding. Alternatively, in screen printing, often a small overlap planned so as to avoid possible gaps of white cloth if registration of the screens is not accurately accomplished.

Plain cotton material used on top of the printing blanket BACK-GREY
to prevent this becoming soiled with excess dye.

A Javanese word for a resist process of patterning cloth. BATIK

A printed ground. BLOTCH

A lightweight, usually knitted, cloth which is strengthened BONDED FABRIC
and thickened by having a lining material fixed to it permanently by means of heat and pressure. Often a very thin layer of foam interlining is placed between two layers of the fabric.

The term used in late Georgian times (when dark printed BOUNDAGE
grounds were in fashion) for the thick edge the block cutter left to his outlines to make the fitting of the background block easier.

The cutting tool (also known as a 'graver') used by a hand BURIN
engraver to incise lines on a copper cylinder or steel die.

Blocks made of type metal, introduced in the 1850s. Many CAST (blocks)
casts of small repeats were made and riveted on to a hardwood base to form a large block. Also known as 'stereo' blocks.

Hindu word meaning coloured and variegated which CHINT
became corrupted in England to 'chintz': a printed floral cotton furnishing fabric on a white or natural ground.

COLOUR BLOCK	A block, usually of wood, infilled with felt to facilitate the printing of bigger areas of colour with as little unevenness as possible.
COLOUR TROUGH	In engraved or surface roller printing, the colour container in which the furnishing brush or roller rotates. Also known as 'colour box'.
COLOURWAY	A rendering of a design or printed fabric in a set of colours differing from the original. Fabrics are usually printed in a set of at least four colourways.
COPPERED BLOCK	A printing block made by hammering in copper or brass strips of varying section.
COPPERING	The art of making coppered blocks.
CURING	See Polymerization.
DECALCOMANIE	An old form of lithographic printing for embroidery transfers. The design was transferred from the tissue paper on which it was printed, usually by ironing; thick enamel-like pigments were used.
DIE	A small cylinder of steel which is hand-engraved with one or more repeats of a small-scale pattern, then hardened and used to produce the mill.
DIRECT STYLE	The type of textile printing in which the mordant and the colouring matter are applied simultaneously. It was very rare until the development of artificial dyestuffs.
DISCHARGE	An agent which removes the colour from previously dyed cloth. Hence the 'discharge style' of printing fabric.
DOCTOR	A traversing steel blade which is placed in contact with the engraved cylinder and serves to scrape off the surplus colour from the raised (non-printing) surface. The term is now applied to any blade-type squeegee.
DRUGS	See Mordants.
DUPLEX	A method of printing in which both sides of the cloth receive the pattern – either at the same time (as with the Aljaba Duplex rotary screenprinting machine) or one side immediately after the other (as in Duplex engraved roller work).
DYED STYLE	A way of patterning cloth in which the design is painted or printed in mordant and subsequently dyed. Only those areas so mordanted take the colour in a fast form.
DYE-PASTE	See Printpaste.

Metal collars fitted to the ends of rotary screens with adhesive. They are given register marks so that each screen can be correctly fitted in position in the printing machine.

END-RINGS

The incising of lines in a metal or other surface by means of a graver or burin. In the textile trade this term is still used even when the pattern rollers are produced by etching or by pressure from the raised surface of a mill in an 'engraving machine'.

ENGRAVING

The craft of producing an intaglio design in metal by means of lines drawn through a thin protective coating (usually of wax) which covers the plate or cylinder; the lines in the exposed metal are then bitten into by acid.

ETCHING

The mechanical method by which the cloth is printed using a number of stationary flat screens of a rectangular shape, working in a line. These screens have colour pressed through the mesh, then they are lifted, the cloth moves on the space of one repeat and the process begins again.

FLAT SCREEN PRINTING

Printing from rubber rollers cut in relief. Introduced in its rotary form in 1963, it is used in the wallpaper industry and is one of the main means of printing transfer paper.

FLEXOGRAPHY

A single stroke (or passage of the squeegee) made while the screens are raised from the table, in flat screen printing. This fills the mesh with printpaste before the screen is lowered to cloth level and the usual squeegee stroke is made; thus in the time of a single stroke almost double the quantity of printpaste is applied to the cloth.

FLOODSTROKE

See Rainbowing.

FONDU

The brush or roller that rotates in the colour trough and supplies the printing roller with colour in engraved cylinder or surface roller printing.

FURNISHING BRUSH (or roller)

Abbreviation for a directly designed galvano screen. The screen mesh and the pattern are 'grown' on a mandrel at one and the same time.

GDD

Also known, in the textile industry, as a 'step-half'. A kind of repeat in which the unit is repeated at a given distance, not directly horizontal but stepped down half its vertical dimension.

HALF-DROP

Printing from flat screens by hand.

HAND SCREEN PRINTING

In photogravure, the system in which the cells are of differing widths but of the same depth.

HARD DOT

A design or line cut into a surface so as to form a hollow or indent.

INTAGLIO

LAPPING	Specially woven fabric which is wound about eight or ten times round the central pressure bowl of a textile printing machine to ensure resilience.
LETTERPRESS	The printing of type or illustrations from an image raised in relief; the surface is inked before being pressed on paper.
LINT DOCTOR	A steel blade positioned at the back of an engraved roller printing machine to scrape off any fluff after printing.
LITHOGRAPHIC PRINTING	Printing (now rarely used directly on to fabric) from pigment colour adhering to a mixed-wax printed pattern on the level surface – as distinct from intaglio or relief images.
LUMP	A measurement of cloth 120 yards long. Also known as a 'piece'.
MAGNET-ROLL SYSTEM	A method whereby squeegees – in the form of cylindrical metal rods, varying in diameter from 3 to 18 mm., placed loosely in the screen with the printpaste – are moved along by means of magnet coils under the printing blanket, which draw the printpaste through the mesh of the screen. It is used in both Johannes Zimmer and Peter Zimmer screen-printing machines.
MANDREL (or mandril)	A supporting steel bar on which the engraved copper cylinder turns.
MATRIX	The form or mould on which something is shaped. In the case of textile printing, it is a solid steel cylinder, or one of inflatable rubber, on which rotary screens are formed.
MILL	A small cylinder of softened steel on which the pattern is raised in relief (by pressure and acid) from contact with a previously engraved die.
MILL ENGRAVING	Also known as 'machine engraving', it is the mechanical method of 'engraving' a cylinder; the design is pressed out by means of a mill.
MORDANT	An agent, often in the form of a metallic oxide, which has an affinity for the cloth and an attraction for the colouring-matter and so in combining with them it forms an insoluble colour lake on the cloth.
NIP	The fixing position for each printing unit in a printing machine of any type. Also known as the 'station'.
PALAMPORES	Indian hand-painted cottons of fairly large size, often patterned with 'Tree of Life' motifs, which were imported into Europe in the seventeenth and eighteenth centuries and used for bedcovers and hangings and later stretched on frames as wall decorations.

A device used to copy a design in a scale other than the original.

PANTOGRAPH

Touching up a printed fabric with a fine brush.

PENCILLING

The machine using the pantograph principle to transfer at one time as many repeats as are required around the surface of the copper cylinder. Originally the design was always increased five times in size on to the zinc master plate before being transferred at original size on to the surface of the copper cylinder – hence this traditional corruption of the word 'pantograph' in the textile trade.

PENTAGRAPH

In the engraved roller industry known as a 'light-sensitive varnish'. It is usually made of a branded PVA (polyvinyl alcohol) emulsion added to a solution of ammonium bichromate. One way, using Stensol (a proprietary brand which is sold unsensitized), is to make a stock solution with 6 per cent sodium bichromate and mix one part stock solution to five parts Stensol.

PHOTOGRAPHIC EMULSION

The process by which an 'engraving' is produced in a metal plate or cylinder by means of light acting on a sensitized surface and the resultant image then being etched in acid. Conventional gravure cylinders all have cells or 'dots' of the same width but varying depth so that they hold either more or less ink, thus producing varying tones of one colour. One of the main methods of printing transfer paper.

PHOTOGRAVURE

Photographic techniques in which a screen serves to break up the gradations of a continuous-tone subject into a series of minute dots of varying size or a series of fine lines.

PHOTOMECHANICAL (techniques)

A style of textile printing (known in France as *picotage*) used in the eighteenth century. A series of brass pins were driven into the surface of the block which was then used to produce a pattern, either as a background or as shadowy shapes of such things as leaves.

PINNING

Fine metal pins driven into the corners of the block for the purpose of establishing the correct repeat.

PITCHES (or pitch pins)

Finding the correct repeat. In engraved roller printing this means putting each roller in correct position while the machine is running slowly. Also known as 'registering' or 'putting in register'.

PITCHING

The chemical union of two or more molecules of the same compound to form larger molecules. In screen printing, the emulsion coating (with added hardener) is baked, or 'cured', to bring about this change – after exposing and developing – as it greatly extends the life of the patterned screen.

POLYMERIZATION

PRESSURE BOWL	The large central cylinder against which the engraved roller rotates and which carries the back-grey and cloth to be printed. Made resilient by lapping, it acts in effect like a print table.
PRINTPASTE	Also known as 'dye-paste'. The blend of colouring-matter, solvents, mordant and thickening which the printer uses to get his impression.
PROCESS ENGRAVING	Known also as 'photographic engraving', in the textile trade this refers to the process in which copper cylinders are etched from 'tracings' (positives) produced entirely by photographic means.
PULL-IN MACHINE	Also known as a 'take-in' machine, this is used to photographically reduce the width of a design as well as for slashing.
PUTTING ON	The job of transferring the design to the surface of the block or die prior to cutting or engraving.
RAINBOWING	Known as 'fondu' in France. The use of a divided colour-box in block printing, so that the colour is transferred to the block in the form of softly shaded stripes.
RAPID AGER	See Ageing.
REGISTRATION	The correct fitting together of all areas and colours in a printed fabric.
REPEAT	The exact reproduction of any unit of design placed in an accurate geometric relationship to it – for instance 'side to side' (known as a 'square' repeat), that is, set at a given distance exactly horizontal and vertical to the original.
RESIST	Wax or a paste of rice or clay painted or printed on to the cloth before dyeing, to reserve a white pattern. There are also modern resists which act chemically to prevent the fixation of the dye. Hence the 'resist style' of printing.
ROTARY SCREEN PRINTING	Printing from a machine equipped with a set of cylindrical screens – usually, but not always, placed in line along a horizontal print table – each fitted with an internal squeegee and colour-feed unit.
RULING MILL	A small mill which has scale lines raised in relief on its surface, and which is used to transfer these lines on to the varnished surface of a copper cylinder.
RULING VARNISH	A specially prepared coating used to protect the surface of the cylinder, but which is malleable enough to be finely and clearly scraped away when the small ruling mill is rotated against it.

A French term (also called 'sanded' or 'vermicular' ground) for a blockprinted cloth which has had tiny pinned dots printed all over it before the printing of the main pattern.

SABLÉ (ground)

In engraved roller work, in order to print a flat area of solid colour, the shape (after outlining) must be filled in with a series of parallel lines set at an angle of between $22\frac{1}{2}$ and $30°$; the number of these to the inch constitutes the scale.

SCALE (lines)

The production of the open and infilled pattern areas on the screen surface; the traditional term is still used, although engraving is in no way involved.

SCREEN ENGRAVING

A form of stencil printing through an open mesh, areas of which have been stopped out to form a pattern.

SCREEN PRINTING

The opaque painted or photographically produced positive of all areas of one design colour on transparent film. Also known as a 'sketch' or 'tracing'.

SEPARATION

The part of the swimming-tub which furnishes the block with colour.

SIEVE

Printing of one side of the cloth only.

SIMPLEX

The controlled distortion necessary to print horizontal stripes by engraved roller. The roller is engraved with the stripes set at an angle of $22\frac{1}{2}$–$30°$ from the horizontal and printed on to cloth stentered off-grain at the same angle. The same effect can be produced photographically on a pull-in machine.

SLASHING

The device (usually in the form of a blade) used to press the printpaste, or alternatively the light-sensitive emulsion, through the mesh of the screen. Also known as a 'doctor'.

SQUEEGEE

A controlled straightening and stretching process. The selvedges of the cloth are attached to a series of pins or clips as it is fed through a machine (or 'stenter'), and as the pins are gradually placed further apart widthways, the cloth is slowly and permanently brought out to the desired width.

STENTERING

A machine which copies as many repeats as are required on to a sensitized screen or film in correct register.

STEP–AND–REPEAT MACHINE

See Half-drop.

STEP–HALF

A copy or cast. In flexographic printing the term is applied to the moulded rubber repeats of the pattern, many of which are fixed together to form a complete roller.

STEREO

In hand engraving, the tonal effects produced by punching small dots on the copper cylinder with a series of small

STIPPLING

punches and hammers. It is no longer practised because gradations can now be more easily produced photographically.

STRIKE-OFF

Sample prints made to prove the accuracy of screens or rollers.

SURFACE ROLLER PRINTING

Rotary printing from cylinders patterned in relief; it was used for traditional chintz to give a hand block effect, but is now seen only in specialist firms and in the wallpaper industry.

SWIMMING-TUB

A wooden tub, half-filled with thickening or old dye-paste to give resilience, over which is stretched a waterproof covering and on which is resting the sieve – a drum stretched over tightly with woollen cloth. The colour is spread on to the sieve and the block pressed against it before printing.

TAB

A raised, straight strip about $\frac{3}{4}$ in. wide and 6–8 in. long cut into the steel collar (which is shrunk into the neck of the steel cylinder) and finally copper coated. Its purpose is to provide a key for locking in the mandrel.

TEARING (or tiering)

The job of spreading the printpaste evenly over the woollen sieve.

THICKENING

Any agent used to 'stodge up' the liquid colouring-matter and to prevent its spread by capillarity to unwanted areas of the cloth. It can be made of natural starches or gums or of artificially made ones.

TJANTING

A tool used exclusively in Java for drawing with wax. It consists of a copper or brass receptacle having one or more spouts, which is mounted on a bamboo or reed handle.

TJAP (block)

A wax printing block made entirely of metal strips and open at the back. It was introduced in the latter half of the nineteenth century to facilitate speedier production in Java.

TOBY PRINTING

A method used in block printing when the different colour areas of a design were clearly separated from each other; the colours were applied by means of a divided sieve and were thus printed at the same time from one block.

TRANSFER PRINTING

A new textile-printing method in which the pattern is printed on to a paper web and transferred by a process of sublimation (under heat and pressure) to fabrics mainly of man-made fibre.

VARNISH

In the textile trade, a term used for any protective coating, light-sensitive or otherwise.

VERMICULAR

See Sablé (ground).

Further reading

CROOKES, W.J.: *Practical Handbook of Dyeing and Calico-printing*. London, 1874.

IRWIN, John, and BRETT, Katharine B.: *Origins of Chintz: with a catalogue of Indo-European Cotton-paintings in the Victoria and Albert Museum, London and the Royal Ontario Museum, Toronto*. London, 1970.

KNECHT, E., and FOTHERGILL, J.B.: *The Principles and Practice of Textile Printing*, 4th ed. London, 1952.

MONTGOMERY, F.M.: *Printed Textiles: English and American Cottons and Linens 1700–1850*. London, 1970.

MORTON, Jocelyn: *Three Generations in a Family Textile Firm*. London and Boston, Mass., 1971.

O'BRIEN, Charles: *The British Manufacturers Companion and Calico Printers Assistant*. London, 1792.

PERCIVAL, MacIver: *The Chintz Book*. 1923, repr. Ann Arbor, Mich., 1972.

SCHOESER, Mary, and RUFEY, Celia: *English and American Textiles: From 1871 to the Present*, London and New York, 1989

THOMPSON, Paul: *The Work of William Morris*. London and New York, 1967.

JOURNALS

Journal of the Society of Dyers and Colourists.
The Ciba Reviews

Index